The
Woo Woo
Book

The Simple Key to Joyous Living
that is Suppressed by Religion and
Ignored by Science

John Ponce

BALBOA.PRESS

A DIVISION OF HAY HOUSE

Balboa Press books may be ordered through booksellers or by contacting:

Balboa Press
A Division of Hay House
1663 Liberty Drive
Bloomington, IN 47403
www.balboapress.com
844-682-1282

Because of the dynamic nature of the Internet, any web addresses or
links contained in this book may have changed since publication and
may no longer be valid. The views expressed in this work are solely those
of the author and do not necessarily reflect the views of the publisher,
and the publisher hereby disclaims any responsibility for them.

The author of this book does not dispense medical advice or prescribe the use
of any technique as a form of treatment for physical, emotional, or medical
problems without the advice of a physician, either directly or indirectly. The
intent of the author is only to offer information of a general nature to help
you in your quest for emotional and spiritual well-being. In the event you use
any of the information in this book for yourself, which is your constitutional
right, the author and the publisher assume no responsibility for your actions.

Any people depicted in stock imagery provided by Getty Images are
models, and such images are being used for illustrative purposes only.
Certain stock imagery © Getty Images.

Print information available on the last page.

ISBN: 979-8-7652-4350-3 (sc)
ISBN: 979-8-7652-4351-0 (e)

Balboa Press rev. date: 09/05/2024

CONTENTS

Foreword.. vii
Introduction.. ix

Part 1: Objections to Woo-woo xv

Chapter 1   Science... 1
Chapter 2   Religion 18
Chapter 3   Modern Culture....................................35

Interlude.. 59

Chapter 4   Five Core Principles to Finding Happiness ...61

Part 2: Woo-woo in Action 91

Chapter 5   How a Woo-woo Mind Feels 93
Chapter 6   Woo-woo is Two Way Communication ... 118
Chapter 7   The Woo-woo Community....................... 151

Closing: What's Next?..173
Acknowledgements..177
Notes 179
Get In Touch With Our Psychics..................................183
More Woo Woo! 185

FOREWORD

It's hard not to sit in awe of *The Woo Woo Book* when the book itself makes you believe in "the Woo" even more than you did *before* you read it.

I am lucky to have manifested John, my tech colleague and friend, a few years ago. After going through the most difficult part of my life, he and I started working together again. He asked if I would read this book and consider writing a foreword for it. Of course, I said yes. Anything for John.

As I was reading it, I started to cry. My life had gotten so unrecognizable and so difficult, and here was my friend's book, telling me that love is the answer, and that I just needed to believe in the Woo again so that I could find my hope. I read the entire book in two sittings. During the second, I took a break mid-way through and meditated effortlessly for the first time in my life.

When I was finished, I opened my eyes to get back to the book. I just happened to be at the part where John recounts our friendship.

I had manifested him once again.

This book is full of resources and stories that can help you align yourself with your greatest good and your most beloved self. You can be a scientist, you can believe in God, and you can work with the Woo. John did it, and his joyful example brought me to tears again and again.

This book was written for you. It's ready for you, just as you are, and the answers you are seeking are just a few pages down the way.

You've got this.

You're exactly where you're supposed to be.

Welcome to *The Woo Woo Book*.

Melissa Cynova xoxo

INTRODUCTION

"Albert Einstein called the intuitive or metaphoric mind a sacred gift. He added that the rational mind was a faithful servant. It is paradoxical that in the context of modern life we have begun to worship the servant and defile the divine." Bob Samples "The Metaphoric Mind: A Celebration of Creative Consciousness" 1976.

Are you on a quest for happiness?

Welcome.

I'm glad you're here.

A recent study on mental health showed that nearly 20% of Americans suffer from depression or severe anxiety.[1] I recall from my high school and college days that I wasn't always happy. I had periods of melancholy that sometimes lasted weeks, even months. I don't know if this counts as severe, but I do know it affected me a great deal during that time.

I worried about a lot of things—grades, fitting in, getting things done, girls, the "normal" stuff. As I got older, those worries changed to making enough money, paying bills, my relationships, and additional responsibilities.

In truth, my life was…well…acceptable. The business that I owned was doing reasonably well. Things weren't amazing, but they weren't terrible either. I had hobbies, friends, some disposable income, things I spent time on. Overall, I had an acceptable life, though an ongoing feeling of ennui, boredom, dissatisfaction, and frustration seemed to permeate almost everything.

Why wasn't I happy? I had nothing to really complain about, but my world felt empty.

Then, in 2015, things got very, very difficult for me. I received the sad news that my dad had been diagnosed with pancreatic cancer. Doctors gave him six months to live, and my siblings and I spent much time discussing various treatments with him—whether chemotherapy would be helpful or just make things more difficult.

In my own family, we were experiencing the joys and challenges of our first child who was one year old at the time. My dad so looked forward to spending time with my son. During our weekly visits together, he would sing to my son, read to him, and just make him giggle. The underlying sadness of knowing my dad had terminal cancer made those times together kind of surreal. Happiness and sadness at the same time.

In June of that year, my dad passed away.

In that same week, I nearly lost my business.

Let's back up for a moment for some context. I have been a business owner for many years, serving my clients with their technology needs. I was instrumental in seeing many of my clients' businesses grow from tiny five-person businesses into multi-million-dollar enterprises with a staff of 30 or 40, moving into bigger buildings and enjoying unparalleled success. My favorite client had started out as a small engineering company but grew into a very successful enterprise; they had great need for technology and were very good about delegating technical decisions to me. I had autonomy to implement best-practice solutions for their company's computer hardware, software, servers, and networks.

There's a rule in business that you never want to have your business reliant on "one." Never have just one supplier, one platform for your ads, one employee, or one solution. And you should never be reliant on just one customer. Well, I *had* other customers, but the engineering firm had grown so big, they now constituted about 60% of my revenue. I felt great pride in being a part of this amazing company's growth and success. And I took great pride in developing and maintaining top-of-the-line technology solutions for them.

Then they fired me.

I was completely blindsided. (In retrospect, there were signs, but I didn't recognize them at the time.) I was called into the CEO's office, and told I was being replaced. The only thing worse than being fired was being fired and not knowing why. I asked what the reason was, and the CEO said, "It wasn't just one thing." End of discussion. Within minutes, I was walking back to my car and leaving that building for the last time.

When you run a business, your expenses need to roughly match your revenues, plus some money set aside as profit. When the income suddenly drops to 40%, the expenses can't be cut as quickly. I had service contracts that I was obligated to pay. I had employees designated to work on that engineering firm's projects. I had equipment that I had paid for that was specifically for that engineering firm's work.

In short, most of my income went away, but my expenses did not. I suddenly realized I was close to bankruptcy.

Somehow, the business survived. We cut other expenses. I took a steep pay cut. Even still, I had to lay off staff members. We worked very hard to make sure our other customers were happy and well cared for.

But my mind was not in great shape. I was frustrated and angry. I felt like a failure. I knew somewhere I had screwed things up but had no idea what truly led to the decision to fire me. I blamed myself for having gotten into such a difficult situation. I lacked any motivation to continue.

I think what kept me going was the support I received from a couple of close friends and colleagues, and that Spirit was watching over me, though this was unknown to me at the time.

I was helped by mentors; I was in a business mentoring program, and my mentor helped me through this most difficult time of my life. I was also in a study group of life coaches where I received wonderful support, kindness, and guidance.

While I acknowledged that I was better off than so many others, I also knew things were not good. As I dwelled on my misery and misfortune, I began to ask questions. *Why did this happen? Why does any disaster happen? How do I know I am going to be OK? Will my family make it through this intact? What can I do now? How do I deal with being so crushed by this? Is there any joy at all in life?*

I began to seek out books about why people are unhappy and what to do about it. This was my first step in my quest for happiness, which ultimately led to going all in on woo-woo.

Bitter or Better

There's a well-known saying that goes something like this: "When you meet calamity, you can either become bitter or better." My road to "better" wasn't assured. I can't think of any good reason why I didn't sink into bitterness and anger except for one thing—I know now that divine guidance (angels?!) was there at every step to ensure I made it through.

I look back on that time as the beginning of my journey. If the whole business disaster hadn't happened, I would have just hummed along in autopilot, living my life not knowing that there was a deeper meaning and not acknowledging that I was brought here for a purpose, as we all are.

This book is about the journey that started as a search for happiness, but soon became the most amazing Spiritual experience, and the joy of my life. I found woo-woo—that weird world of people who talk to Spirits, who read Tarot, who heal with their hands, and who have a pervasive peace around them all the time.

My journey was mostly through books and courses that I discovered along the way. I have found an immense power and beauty in the community aspect of this experience and believe that through sharing our experiences we can connect more deeply with one another.

I aim here to share the path that I took, and the books and teachers that I learned from that were so helpful to me. I refer to many books—my own personal guides—which you can use to dive deeper into a particular topic. Find the woo-woo that excites you and go all in.

Once you are on your path to woo-woo, I invite you to then, in turn, share what you have learned with others. Through this cycle of learning and sharing we can continue to strengthen our collective experience and impact.

Our Journey Together

In Part One of this book, I present the objections to woo-woo and respond to them with books and convincing research. If you are on the fence about woo-woo, I hope you will be *all in* after this section or at least have more to ponder.

I share five core principles of woo-woo. I describe how woo-woo affected me, my personality, and the joy it brought to me once I realized what life was all about. What changes inside you when you embrace intuition, Spirit, and let go of the need to *do* instead of just *be*?

In Part Two, we'll dig into the many ways we can interact with Spirit—through healing, through intuitive questions, through signs, magic, and community. These are all tools you can choose to explore on your path.

My journey has been through reading and research, so throughout the book I describe many of the masters whom I learned from and the books I read to bring me along this path.

How many people do you know who are *truly* happy? Let's increase that number by one as you experience this new joy of living—living in this state of woo-woo.

PART 1

. . . .

Objections to Woo-woo

CHAPTER ONE

....

SCIENCE

One of my first memories of childhood is of visiting a neighbor's house with my parents. There was a lamp with a cord that went under a rug in the living room, and I remember slowly and carefully pulling up the rug (with everyone watching and laughing) to see where the cord went. I followed the length of the cord to the outlet on the wall and was satisfied that I had found the starting point. Cords and wires—and making sense of the world—fascinated me from an early age.

Other early elementary school age memories are of my dad and I spending hours together building various circuits with a battery, a light bulb, and switches.

In college, I got my degree in computer science, and went on to write software for several companies. I then started and ran a computer tech support business for many years.

I am (or was) all tech.

I'm a product of two parents with PhDs: both taught in universities, and both were authors. My sister is a doctor, my brother is a research chemist, and my other sister is a veterinarian.

Intellectual pursuits pervade our family.

We were also a religious family. My dad was a pastor for his entire career, and both parents participated fully in the church and the well-known university associated with our Christian denomination.

For these reasons, I have a unique perspective on why someone might object to the world of woo-woo.

Some Quick Context

What's "woo-woo" again? Well, woo-woo is the term often used to describe the using of your intuition, learning to listen to the messages of the Spiritual side; it's ESP, it's healing bodies by laying on of hands, it's speaking to Spirits, it's reading Tarot cards to get an answer to a burning question.

The world of woo-woo is at odds with my intellectual upbringing and at odds with my Christian upbringing.

And yet, I am all in on woo-woo.

I see three main objections to woo-woo—those rooted in the intellectual, in the religious, and in modern culture. We'll talk about each, one chapter at a time.

Intellectuals scoff at woo-woo because it isn't scientific. (Actually, it is, but we'll get to that.) Established religion shuns woo-woo because it is forbidden. (Also not true, but we'll get there, too.) And modern life keeps us distracted and annoyed, such that we have no knowledge that there might be a better way, and seemingly no time to explore it.

For me, woo-woo is why we are here on this planet. Woo-woo is what brought me to immeasurable peace in my life, it even changed my personality. With woo-woo, I can be calm and patient in the face of stress and difficult situations. And it has brought such joy and happiness to my life, I can hardly contain it!

The Beginning

We'll begin with scientific objections, but I want to take a quick pause and provide a little context on my religious upbringing, as much of these conversations are intertwined.

I was brought up in a Protestant religious household. Discussions of faith and religion were part of the fabric of my family. My Christian heritage gave me a strong moral compass but also the permission to ask hard questions and challenge teachings and assumptions.

The beginning of my Spiritual journey started with a search for happiness. At that time, many questions began going through my mind; one question was the question of faith, religion, and God. It's the big "What if" question— what if this whole religion thing was a construct of our own minds? What if it's not true?

I think part of "growing up" as a human being is making decisions about your beliefs—that is, "What do I believe, and why do I believe it?" When I began to search for Truth, I began to question everything. I questioned what I had been taught growing up, both Christianity and religion in general. Was any of it really true or had I just accepted everything I had been handed?

What if there isn't a God? What if the idea of a soul is just an imaginary thing? What if we're just a brain in a body?

What if when we die, that's the end?

I took that last question seriously. I started thinking about all the assumptions that a religious upbringing provided and, for the first time in my life, I became open to considering the possibility that churches and religious groups might be a huge waste of time and energy. Maybe religious organizations were all talking about something imaginary.

Sure, the social programs of churches were good, and the teachings of being a better person were helpful, but the premise of a soul or Spirit suddenly seemed like complete fiction. In the beginning of my journey, these questions were some of the most challenging to grapple with.

I vividly remember sitting in church during the most difficult part of my life and hearing the pastor speak about what God wants us to do. I was thinking, *do you really know God? And do you really know what he wants us to do? How absurd. We don't even know our next-door neighbors, let alone know "God."*

As I watched religious disagreements in the news and read of modern wars and attacks over whose version of God was correct, it all seemed even more ridiculous.

If God doesn't exist, and if the soul doesn't exist, then we're expending a whole lot of energy on nothing. I remember the realization washing over me that a huge portion of my upbringing and of my present life were potentially meaningless.

Imagine all the resources and energy put into building churches, ordaining ministers, debating scripture, writing commentaries, studying minute differences in language in this scripture versus that scripture. Then think of all the other world religions with their buildings of worship, clergy, scriptures, debates, and discussions! A huge amount of energy and resources for imaginary things!

As I grappled with this conclusion, it wasn't all bad. In one way, this realization made life easier. I didn't have to worry about an afterlife, or what I should be doing or commandments or any set of rules.

I just had to create a reasonably comfortable life for myself, not hurt anyone else, get through to old age without a major screw-up or painful disease, and I'd be OK. Easy, right?

In another way, though, I was sad to see this part of my life dry up. I had been brought up in a Christian home, with Christian parents, an outstanding education in a Christian school, and having most of my relatives in missions or the ministry.

Science played a part in this struggle, too. I had read enough science books and articles to know that modern scientists had figured out a lot of how the brain works and found no evidence of a soul or Spirit.

Many so-called religious experiences could be simulated with chemicals; dopamine, oxytocin, serotonin, and endorphins were all measurable and linked to happiness.

God and soul were constructs of our own minds, tools used by religions to keep us in line, and focused on getting through life. If the soul and God weren't real, what was the source of happiness?

Well, wasn't I too stressed and worried about day-to-day life to find out?!

It suddenly seemed as though the major foundations of my life—religion, scientific inquiry, and many aspects of the modern world around me—were leaving me stranded. I knew I wasn't really happy with my life, and suddenly realized that I only had this one life to enjoy. I'd better make the most of it, and I needed to figure out how to do so.

What do you do when you need to figure something out? Well, I began reading books on happiness. What does it take to become happy?

The solutions presented in books were all over the map— happiness was elusive, it could be achieved by regimen, it was only found in human relationships, or it could be achieved by service to others. There are many, many books on creating or discovering happiness.

The idea of a "brain in a body" concept stuck with me until I read one particular book and my journey to self-discovery took off.

A Brain in a Body

I've always been interested in psychology and especially the idea of ESP. In college, my psychology class did the standard ESP experiment where you try to guess or sense the symbol that your partner is mentally sending you. Our class paired off, and with my partner, I got them all wrong. Not the 25% correct that you'd get statistically. I got them *all* wrong. Clearly, I had no extra sensory perception whatsoever. It was a big disappointing moment for me.

As I began to explore, my biggest shift in understanding happened when I read *Entangled Minds: Extrasensory Experiences in a Quantum Reality* by Dean Radin.[1]

I heard about this book because it was mentioned briefly in a business and marketing newsletter I had subscribed to. The newsletter mentioned in just one small paragraph that "the world is a much more interesting place than it appears to be. Don't believe for a minute that we've figured everything out already."

That might be a key concept for life: Don't believe for a minute that we've figured everything out. If we can approach life with that kind of curiosity and openness, we will constantly experience new miracles.

I studied *Entangled Minds*, and it completely changed my view on brains, minds, connections between minds, and a whole lot of things. Radin lays out the case for extrasensory reality, and then goes on to explain how it might happen via quantum fields.

Radin gives example after example of individuals knowing the future, reading minds, unexplained connections between individuals, and so on. But not just examples; he gives laboratory tests that prove the findings are more than chance. Real science.

The difference between many woo-woo books and Radin's book is that Radin cites scientific double-blind experiments that detail the existence of some kind of mind connection between test subjects.

I was blown away by these examples. Why hadn't I heard about these experiments before? This changed everything for me.

Two such experiments he shares illustrate the amazing things our minds can do.

The first example is an experiment to measure the ability of one individual to communicate with another over distance using the mind (also known as telepathy). Keep in mind that this experiment is carried out with proper rigorous scientific method standards.

In the experiment, two researchers begin in different buildings far apart, such that there is no clear line of sight between the buildings. One researcher has a stack of cards with images on them known as Zener cards. The deck of cards is shuffled, and the cards are placed one at a time face down. For each card, the first researcher tries to perceive what the image is without looking and then "sends" his perceived image of that card to the other researcher who writes down the message he receives.

The results were very interesting. This experiment showed that the recipient guessed correctly by a small but significant percentage higher than chance. Even more interesting is that when the experiment was repeated, each time the findings were the same; the number of correct images was slightly over the number that could be attributed to chance. This means that *something* caused the image to be recorded correctly more often than chance.

A second example is an experiment on presentiment. The person (called the test subject) is connected to a device that measures the body's reaction to seeing an image. When peaceful or happy images are displayed, the stress response is minimal or non-existent, and the device measures that reaction. If the image is disturbing or frightening, the body's stress response is clear and measurable.

The test subject was shown numerous images randomly, and the stress reaction was measured for each image. As we would expect, the measured stress reaction was higher for the disturbing images; however, the significant thing is that this experiment showed that the reaction happened slightly *before* the image was shown. Why before? That's the mystery. The research showed that the test subject was able to know slightly in advance what kind of image would be shown.

I'll address the topic of how the scientific community reacted to experiments like this a bit later. For now, keep in mind that the experiments each followed the necessary scientific method and have been peer-reviewed.

What I learned from Radin was that as humans, being just a "brain in a body" did not explain our experiences fully.

Science has shown that there are a few phenomena that exist in humans that aren't part of our five senses. If these unusual phenomena truly exist, then there might be something more than just brains in bodies. It must be brain, body, and something. This made me think: *Well, if that's true, then the idea of a soul or consciousness might be related, and that requires some more explanation.*

Like many, I previously held on to the idea that science—as a discipline—was enough to prove we have no Spirit. Because of *Entangled Minds*, I was able to accept the idea of consciousness which led me to a deep exploration into mind-body connections, consciousness and ultimately set me on the next steps of my Spiritual journey. I am deeply grateful to Mr. Radin for his research. It is a wonderful reminder to all of us that we still have a long way to go to learning everything there is to know about mind and body.

Bad Science

Not everyone is as big of a fan as I am. Dean Radin's research brought up example after example of studies with conclusive findings on communication happening outside of the five senses, knowing of the future, and other related topics. These findings were then dismissed or panned in some way by other "scientists."

The problem is that much of science today has a pretty strong assumption about how the universe operates. That is, we already know about the electromagnetic, gravitational, and other forces in the world, and we know that humans have five senses, so any evidence that might challenge these assumptions is clearly wrong.

Right?

There's one renegade scientist in this conversation about science whom I like very much—Rupert Sheldrake. In *Science Set Free*, Sheldrake takes the scientific community to task.[2] He states that the biggest scientific delusion is that science has all the answers. Looking back over the last few hundred years, Sheldrake points out that science has brought us enormous benefits and gains, through better diets, food production, medicine, communication, transportation, and the many wonders we experience in modern life. But the delusion is that our world is completely physical, and anything that cannot be measured in the physical world is not real.

Modern science even defines consciousness (that is, *our souls*) as a byproduct of brain activity—nothing more than chemical interactions.

Sheldrake is very pro-science. The scientific method is what got us to our current level of sophisticated technology. But the belief system that modern science is based on is what Sheldrake is speaking against.

Sheldrake lists ten core beliefs that most scientists take for granted. Some of them include the belief that everything is a mechanism and that even people are just sophisticated machines. Another is that nature is purposeless, and another is that memories are stored in the brain and wiped out after death. The best one on the list is that unexplained phenomena, such as ESP, are illusory.

Sheldrake rightly points out that by believing these ten points, modern science must discount evidence to the contrary. And, when you discount evidence, you're not really doing good science.

Famous Writers and Scientists Support Psychic Work

I've read about a funny secret among scientists today. If you ask some scientists privately, off the record, about psychic phenomena, connecting with relatives who have passed away or other woo-woo topics, many will concede that they believe in it and find it very interesting. But on the record, almost none of them will admit to it. In other words, many scientists today privately believe in the soul and in psychic phenomena but are unwilling to say so publicly. To do so would be to end their careers in science.

However, there are some notable exceptions. The writer Upton Sinclair who wrote *The Jungle* also wrote extensively about psychic abilities, most notably his wife's work as a psychic.[3] Albert Einstein was very intrigued by a psychic named Gene Dennis, and publicly endorsed Sinclair's work on psychic matters.[4] Thomas Edison worked on a "Spirit phone" device that would allow the living to communicate with the dead. Nikola Tesla worked on a similar device.[5]

A Stolen Harp and Remote Viewing

Through my research I found several other books and papers that reinforced the point that ESP and psychic abilities were real and were being used in the real world.

Remote Viewing Secrets was written by Joseph McMoneagle, a member of the U.S. Army's clairvoyance program.[6] I learned that the United States government employed individuals with psychic abilities to help in intelligence gathering operations. That says a lot right there. Regardless of how vehemently the scientific community might oppose the idea of psychic abilities, the government saw results as the measure of its worth. In other words, while traditional science said it was all trickery and fraud, the U.S. Army believed in and employed capable remote viewers— psychics who could "see" things remotely.

I greatly enjoyed this research, and learned much about

how remote viewers were tested, vetted, and trained. I was amazed at what they were able to accomplish.

The Army project was referred to as Project STARGATE and was kept a secret for about 20 years. It was discontinued in 1995, but remote viewers are still being employed by companies and individuals.

A typical remote viewing session would include the remote viewer and another individual who would take notes on the session. A remote viewer would first get into a calm mind state, and then be given instructions by the assistant to "view" a particular target. The remote viewer would then describe in as much detail as possible what he or she was seeing, details about the surroundings, objects, colors and so on.

Beginner remote viewers would be able to describe shapes and shadows, but advanced viewers could literally describe an entire scene in complete detail.

The book is a fascinating exploration into the systematic use of psychic abilities and describes many of the polarizing arguments of this skill, including how it worked, how it can be used, and whether or not it *should* be used.

For me, it was one more example of how the world was much more interesting and miraculous than I had previously believed.

Speaking of books with huge impact: scientist Elizabeth Lloyd Mayer penned *Extraordinary Knowing*, centering a powerful personal experience.[7] "In December of 1991, my daughter's harp was stolen," Mayer begins. "We got it back. But it came back in a way that irrevocably changed my familiar world of science and rational thinking."

The story goes like this: Following the theft, Mayer

spends months trying to recover the antique harp using "normal" means—the police, rare instrument dealers, and so on, but is unable to locate it.

After nearly giving up, a friend of hers says, "If you are willing to try anything to get it back, you should call a dowser," someone practicing a type of divination using special rods or pendulums.

Mayer is a scientist and professor. She describes her life in vivid detail and shares how she has no time for dealing with "crackpot pseudo-science." But, almost as a dare, she locates and calls a dowser—President of the American Society of Dowsers as it turns out. The dowser (living thousands of miles away) requests a map of her city. Soon, he reports back the cross streets where the harp is located. Through a series of posters, messages, phone calls and a late-night dark-alley meeting, the harp is returned to her.

That's just the beginning of the book. The rest of the book is Mayer's wrestling with this strange occurrence. How could this be possible? It doesn't fit with our scientific understanding of the world.

She describes how much of mind-matter research is shoddy and poorly done. But she also finds very excellent science and research into these phenomena. Mayer profoundly states: "Yet as I delved more deeply, what most impressed me was the significant bank of well-conducted, scientifically impeccable research that imposes enormous questions on anyone interested in making sense of the world from a Western scientific point of view."

The book is the result of her own exploration into the research of psychic abilities. Mayer's experience and exploration helped firm up for me that I was on the right path. If these "odd" things were true, then I knew I was something more than a brain in a body. My mechanistic view of life had crumbled. How could this be? There was proof that we have abilities to sense things beyond our five senses,

Once more, I wondered: why hadn't I been told about this before?

More Science

I want to close here where I began this part of my journey: with *Entangled Minds*. Radin takes a good portion of this book to describe how there is a very strong bias against ESP-types of studies. They get lumped together with UFOs and other crackpot science. Funding for these types of studies is almost impossible to find.

But Radin also points out how rigorously and carefully the experiments are conducted; in fact, ESP-types of studies are held to a higher standard than other kinds of experiments. They need to account for all kinds of potential bias, they need to prevent any possible hint of fraud or trickery, the math and statistical analysis must be perfect, and so on. Even then, the studies are most often dismissed by the conventional scientific community.

One favorite argument against ESP-types of studies is that conventional science will claim that studies that *do not* show ESP to be valid are *not* published, but studies that *do* show ESP to be valid *are* published. Radin takes on this argument as well by showing several meta-studies that examine hundreds of studies on ESP and related topics. The conclusion is once again—No. The less-than-favorable studies are *not* being hidden away in a drawer somewhere. They just don't exist.

ESP, telepathy, clairvoyance, and similar fields are controversial to mainstream thought. When you read about these concepts for the first time, you might have one of three reactions.

First, you might dismiss the possibility completely because, well, this stuff just can't happen. Right? You might be a hardened skeptic and would quickly dismiss the entire subject.

Secondly, you might look for holes in the story to justify your conclusion that this stuff doesn't happen; you would be convinced that the science is flawed, the researchers were sloppy, or they were deliberately fraudulent in their experiment. You would spend time explaining all the possible ways the experiments were done incorrectly. You would be assured of your position because science shows what is possible and what is not possible. (Never mind that you are willing to discard evidence that doesn't support your own beliefs.)

The third possibility would be that you might keep an open mind and think "That's really odd, and it doesn't jive with what I've been taught, but I sure wonder how that might actually work. Wow."

As for me, my current reaction is "Yes, of course. That's how the woo-woo world works." But it took me a while to get there.

I recently had a conversation with a group of friends about a para-psychology article I had just read. I described the article to them and commented on how amazing it was. One of my friends, Jack, was adamant that it could not be true because "science said so." In his opinion, there had to be another explanation: the experiment was biased, or the experiment lacked good experiment controls, or the researchers made conjectures, and so on. Jack's conclusion was made before he had heard the whole story. He also refused to even consider reading the article. He "knew" what was right and had no need to hear other evidence.

If you start with your conclusion, you'll always end up fitting the evidence into your view of how things work.

When confronted with something that doesn't fit our beliefs or view of the world, we have a few options. We can deny it. Whatever claim is being made is false. We can explain it away. Maybe bad record-keeping or misperceptions. Or, we can say "What if this really is true? Let's explore it and see what we can find out."

That's what we can do here together.

CHAPTER TWO

. . . .

RELIGION

A few years ago, my company was doing business with a church. One day, I was talking to one of the staff members of the church. She was a very giving person, generous to everyone she knew, and very kind. She embodied many of the principles of giving and receiving love. We got on the topic of how to deal with difficulties in life and how to not let words from others bother us. I mentioned that I spend time every day in meditation, letting go of thoughts of resistance and judgment. Surprisingly, she responded abruptly. "Oh, now *that* sounds a little too 'new-agey' for me, and I'm not sure I like that."

Bam. Our conversation was over. I've remembered that interaction ever since as I mull over how our pre-conceived notions of what we're allowed and not allowed to believe cause us to dismiss essential Truth with a mere label.

Her message: *Oh, you are talking about something that I label a New Age idea. I believe that New Age ideas are wrong. Therefore, you must be wrong and we need to stop talking.*

I did not have an opportunity to dig into her perspective

further, but if I had, with hindsight, I could have responded with "Oh, tell me more about that. What about New Age ideas make you uncomfortable?" My purpose there would just be to listen and learn. I wonder if, like me many years ago, the staff member had a view about my practices as a New Age concept or a fundamental belief in Christianity that was based on dogma rather than essential Truth.

Sola Scriptura

In 1517, a Catholic church scholar named Martin Luther publicly posted a list of 95 objections to some of the teachings of the Catholic Church. Many of his objections were spot on, having to do with how money was being used in the church. But one of his theses had some unintended consequences.[8]

Luther spoke of "sola scriptura," which is Latin for "only scripture." Essentially, he was saying that the only way we can know if something is from God is if it is found in scripture. Many of the teachings of the church back then were *not* from scripture, they were traditions that had developed over time. Some were definitely off track, and others were just cultural traditions.

Luther's 95 theses began the Reformation, where large groups of believers broke away from the Catholic church, reforming teachings in the process.

The unintended consequence of "sola scriptura" is that many of the Christian traditions dismissed any Spiritual experience that wasn't explicitly found in the Bible as a result. That is the tradition that I grew up in.

My own religious upbringing was very cerebral and

intellectual. Our pastors and leaders were scholars and thinkers. The mind and education were held in high regard.

Spiritual experiences, not so much.

The idea that we might actually receive a message from God or from a Spirit on the other side was pretty unusual, and often dismissed as wishful thinking or as something evil.

I recall that my dad preached a sermon one day in which he addressed the issue of "asking God for a sign." He told the story of someone who was deep in discussion with a close friend and needed to know what God's will was for him. In his mind, he prayed for a sign, and at that moment, the friend inexplicably blew out the candle on the table. The point of the sermon was that in very special circumstances you may ask God for a sign. If you are fortunate, you might receive one.

Looking back, I know that I remember that sermon for a reason. I now realize that the whole point of our lives is to be in communion with a higher power. Not only may we ask for signs any time, but we are also receiving signs all the time! It's our job to pay attention.

Religious Objections are Not Based in Fact

Now, in the realm of the religious discussion, my point is not to enter directly into the middle of any specific debate; however, I do believe it's important to point out that some of our beliefs in the origins of scripture might be incorrect.

Bart Ehrman is an expert who has had a huge influence on my perspectives on modern Christianity. Two pivotal works by him are *Jesus, Interrupted* and *How Jesus Became*

God.[9] The book *Jesus, Interrupted* shows how the books of the Bible's New Testament were decided upon, and who made the decisions to include some books and not others. As Christianity was just forming, there were competing interpretations of the divinity of Jesus—was he *God and man*, or *a man with God-like properties*, or *just God*? Other gospels were being written at the same time as the ones we know in the Bible, and these other gospels were excluded based on some suspect reasoning and the agenda of the decision-makers. The *Gospel of Thomas* is one of those books.

The decision on which books to include and which ones to exclude was done by a committee and the committee had *already decided* which interpretation of the divinity of Jesus was the correct one. That decision made the decision of which books to keep for the "official"—canonical—scripture pretty simple. "If the book agrees with our interpretation, it stays; if it doesn't, it goes."

Interestingly, many of the "rejected" writings of the time are more in line with our understanding of the divine nowadays. One element of the rejected writings is the belief that humans all have a divine spark or piece of God inside them and need to be awakened to that presence; this concept is close to that of Zen Buddhism.

Who Wrote the Scriptures?

I learned many things reading Ehrman's writings. I was amazed to learn that none of the books of the New Testament were written by writers who actually knew Jesus. Most people assume that Matthew, Mark, and John were written by the disciples with those names. As it turns out, all four of the gospels were written without ascribing them to a particular author. It is assumed that readers in that time knew who wrote them, but as for us modern readers, we do not know for sure. Church leaders ascribed the names to the gospels many years later. In fact, all the gospels were written many years after Jesus' death. Stories circulated in the oral tradition for decades before anyone wrote them down. Imagine how a story might be affected by forty years of oral tradition!

Many of early Christianity's symbols and writings were borrowed from other religious groups. One of the most interesting symbols is the Sator Square, a series of five Latin words arranged in a square, which can be read forward, backward, up, and down. The letters can also be arranged to spell "pater noster," which is Latin for "Our Father." You might recognize that as the beginning of the Lord's prayer. The Sator Square was first thought to be an early Christian symbol, but it was discovered in Pompeii dating back to pre-Christian influence there. The point is that the Sator Square and the words of the Lord's prayer may have circulated in other religious groups prior to Christianity. The borrowing of symbols and ideas was common. How much of what we read in the Bible was borrowed from the culture of the time? It's hard to say for sure, but there is some evidence for it. Writers back in the times of early Christianity might have written religious books anonymously or they might have ascribed someone else's name to the books to give them more authority. There is much controversy in the world of early church scholarship as to whether all the books ascribed to the apostle Paul were actually written by him.

I write this not to be disrespectful of the Bible or Christianity. You can—and should—read Ehrman's books to get a perspective on the Bible and how early Christianity formed. I write this to emphasize that many of our own fundamental beliefs might be mistaken or are based on facts that aren't really facts.

And if some of our facts aren't true, that means we can really have an open mind about our religious beliefs. Maybe some of our beliefs are based on assumptions. There are greater Truths (with a capital T) that transcend all religions.

Given this lack of divine truth, when you hear objections to the idea of being able to connect to Spirit and intuition *"because the Bible says,"* (that is, based on dogmatic beliefs in established religious traditions) then I simply ask you to keep an open mind. Take another look.

Heaven and Hell

My Christian upbringing taught that the soul was real and that at the end of life we would be in heaven; however, only after my journey into a Spiritual life did that truth really hit home for me.

As I mentioned, the version of Christianity that I grew up in focused very much on an intellectual understanding of the Bible, theology, and learning every bit that we could about Jesus and the truths taught in the Bible. But we did not focus on the Spiritual aspect of Christianity and were suspicious of other denominations that did claim to have Spiritual experiences.

I went to a private Christian school all my academic years. I recall one time in school we were discussing miracles found in the Bible in religion class and one student asked why there were miracles in the Bible but not today. The instructor answered that clearly God worked in the world one way in the past but no longer does so in the present. Looking back, I see that this idea is mistaken on so many levels. There *are* miracles today, God has *not* changed how he interacts with the world, and a religion that denies our own Spiritual nature and Spiritual abilities is suppressing the most amazing part of our human experience! For me, it took a soul journey to discover these amazing truths.

The two leaders in this field, Anita Moorjani and Brian Weiss, are very clear that *everyone* reaches the beautiful Spiritual state after death. (More on them both in a bit.) In other words, heaven is for all, and there is no hell.

That brings me back to Bart Ehrman. Ehrman's books are at the same time controversial and matter of fact. Erhman is a historian who focuses on the years from the time when Jesus was born through the following 300 or 400 years. He explains how the New Testament books of the Bible that tell the stories of Jesus were written 50 years after Jesus' death and how none of them are eye-witness accounts of the stories of Jesus. So many things in the New Testament books are either contradictory or written with a completely different point of view. For me, this was all eye-opening news. Erhman explains that these facts about the Bible are well known in theological circles but not so well known by the average churchgoer.

In *Jesus, Interrupted* and in Ehrman's blog, he makes a little bit of fun of the idea of hell: "The Lake of Fire is stoked up and ready for everyone who is opposed to God. This will involve *eternal* burning…Twenty trillion years of torment in exchange for twenty years of wrong living; and that's only the beginning. Is this really worthy of God?"[10]

Jesus, Interrupted explains that much of what modern-day Christians take as fact is likely not fact. Human decisions are much more responsible for the contents of our Bible than most people realize. That made me realize that we can and should take a bit less of an intellectual approach to Christianity and more of a get-to-the-heart-of-truth approach. What is the central core teaching of the Bible? Love others. Listen to Spirit. Heal bodies and hearts.

Translations are Never Perfect

In early 2022, I was made aware of a documentary that was in the works in which the controversy over a particular Bible translation was discussed. The movie describes how the word "homosexual" entered into a translation of the Bible in 1946. Amazingly, that word was never in any Bible translation prior to that date. The original Greek texts do not contain that word, but the team responsible for translating a particular section of the Bible decided to combine two independent words into the word "homosexual" in the Revised Standard Version translation of the Bible. The section of the Bible in question gives a list of behaviors that are not godly and asserts people who engage in those behaviors will not be accepted by God.

There were several people on the translation team who opposed this decision, but in the end the team's decision was to keep the word in. The documentary goes on to describe how this has become ingrained into our modern culture, effectively labeling gays as despised by God—all because of a mistranslation of a word.

Another example: in other parts of the New Testament (Galatians 5:20), "sorcery" is translated from the Greek word pharmakeia, where we get our word pharmacy. The word pharmakeia literally means "the use of medicine, drugs or spells." The historical context of that is that the practice of pharmakeia involved the making of herbal concoctions—some of them poisons—meant to harm others. Why lump all woo-woo together with things meant to harm others? The translation of "sorcery" was a decision made by translators.

My point here with these examples is simply this: decisions made by humans are responsible for the beliefs of an established religion. Humans are fallible. Therefore, our translations are never perfect.

Casting Lots

The Bible is full of examples, in both Old and New Testament, where God's people "cast lots" to determine his will. We don't know the exact method used for casting lots but, most likely, it was a practice of using items from nature (bones, stones, sticks), throwing them in a bowl or cloth, and determining the meaning based on patterns of the items thrown. Why is this significant? Because the casting of lots was well known, used frequently, and encouraged by the faithful. Casting lots was a sacred act used to help determine the will of God. Casting lots begins with a prayer and ends with a decision blessed by God.

How might casting lots look in the modern world? How about a ceremony that begins with a prayer, an individual drawing from a stack of oracle cards, and a determination of meaning based on the cards drawn? A sacred act used to help determine the will of God.

My point here is that what is considered "good" divination or "bad" divination is very subjective. In the world of woo-woo, a space I am now deeply entrenched, we seek to help others, bring joy and love to the world, and we cast lots (use divination) to determine the will of Spirit with gratitude.

A Deep Knowing

So, why *do* people think that religion conflicts with woo-woo? The simplistic answer they give is that woo-woo (in their minds) is considered from somewhere other than God. Some claim that since meditation isn't in scripture, it must be "of the devil."

But I would argue that the essence of woo-woo is already part of deep religious traditions; in fact, they're probably already doing it.

Throughout history, Christian contemplatives have long used the chant and deep contemplation to pray and connect with God. Christian mystics practiced this meditative kind of prayer and taught meditation to their followers. At some points in history, it was almost an "underground" kind of movement, but it has been there in the Christian tradition all along.

Meditation *is* a strong component of the established religion. Only modern-day Christians have forgotten about it.

I love how this practice of meditation is being rediscovered in our modern life. Starting from the 1960's, the practices of meditation and contemplation are coming from Eastern cultures back over to our Western culture. And now many Christian denominations wholly embrace these practices and are finding out that they have been part of the Christian tradition all along.

A deeply religious friend of mine and I were having a conversation about her recent job search and her struggles with finding a career that was fulfilling. She mentioned that while contemplating this, she suddenly had a "deep knowing" that she would find just the right job. I pressed her a bit on this point, and she very quietly said "God spoke to me. I just knew." Later that turned out to be true.

That deep knowing goes by other names—some call it intuition, some acknowledge it is the Spirit talking, or a being given a word from God. This skill of listening to Spirit, of honing our intuition—this is the single most important part of woo-woo. It is part of who we are as humans and cannot be explained away by science or wished away by religious dogma.

The Eternal Soul: What Happens After Death?

When I was young, I remember often asking my dad what heaven would be like, and the answer was always "We don't really know." In a sense that was true. At the time, there weren't many stories about near-death experiences. But even if there were, those experiences would likely have been dismissed as fiction or delusional by parents and teachers.

By insisting that the only valid Spiritual information comes from the Bible, many of us have cut ourselves off from the very real experiences of Spirit—both our own experiences and those of others who have written about it. I find this the worst part about growing up in the intellectual version of Christianity that I did.

While I acknowledge the benefits of having a strong foundation for Spiritual beliefs, I also believe that going too far in that direction can eliminate the possibility of receiving your own revelation. Having a written "scripture" on which to base our Spiritual beliefs prevents being swayed by the various random teachings that come and go. A written document is the litmus test to see if something aligns with our beliefs or not. But the problem with that is clear—it remains static and is not open to new information; it's nearly impossible to update the written text.

Could there be Truth that we learn now that wasn't available to writers of scripture a couple thousand years ago? Clearly, I believe the answer is "yes."

I would contend that we are barely scratching the surface as to what our Spiritual selves can experience! In our modern world, we continue to see example after example of amazing Spiritual experiences that people have.

We've now seen that our conscious selves extend beyond our physical bodies through examples of mind connections, remote viewing experts, dowsing and so on.

Our consciousness can connect with others, "see" things far away and do all sorts of amazing things. This consciousness outside our bodies *is* the soul. And when our bodies die, the soul remains.

For me, the logical step-by-step of learning what is possible, seeing what others are able to do, and understanding experiments and tests—all of this has led me to understand that we have souls or Spirits that do not die.

What does happen at the end of our lives, then? If the death of the body isn't the end, what is it?

One work on this topic stands out—*Dying to Be Me* by Anita Moorjani.[11] Moorjani grew up in a multicultural environment with many obligations, fears, and concerns, culminating in a dreaded cancer diagnosis, followed by months of intense suffering.

The eye-opening surprise is when Moorjani details her last day in the hospital on her death bed. She suddenly finds herself above her bed looking down and able to hear, see and experience her surroundings in amazing ways. She describes seeing the bright light, relatives inviting her into the beyond and a decision to make on whether to return to earth or leave her body permanently. Armed with a new life's purpose, she decides to return.

Moorjani had what is known as a near-death experience or NDE. She was unfamiliar with the concept prior to her own experience, but later connected with others who had similar experiences, as well as with researchers who study NDEs. Because of modern science and the ability to hold bodies between life and death, the experience of an NDE has become more common. The NDE simply adds to our rich deepening understanding of our Spiritual selves. We haven't even begun to explore this fully!

Moorjani eloquently teaches many of the same principles that I have described here: living a life of joy, non-judgment of others, and living fully in the present.

Through spending time with her story, Moorjani reminded me that our fears and anxieties are unnecessary, that life is meant to be joyful and that we just need to trust that the Universe, God, Source—however you name the higher power—is here for you. We are not here to judge others; we are here to live lives of joy.

What About Reincarnation?

If our soul exists prior to our earthly lives *and* exists after our death, then is it possible that we might have had more than one earthly life?

Buddhism and several other religions include reincarnation as a central tenet of the faith.

Another pioneer in this field is Brian Weiss, who wrote *Many Lives, Many Masters* and other related books.[12] His amazing life story is as a very scientific person—a psychologist—who is thrown into a situation where a Spiritual truth is discovered. As a scientist, Weiss studies, tests ideas, takes careful research notes and presents his carefully documented findings in a matter-of-fact way.

Many Lives, Many Masters is the story of one of his patients, Catherine, who comes to him for help with panic attacks that she has been experiencing. Weiss suggests using hypnosis to uncover the root of the panic attacks. During one of the hypnosis treatments, Catherine starts talking about life in an ancient civilization, difficulties of daily life and specific details of her life in that civilization. Weiss is very surprised at this; he tries to explain it clinically, but eventually realizes the details have no good explanation.

Weiss proceeds to record and document these sessions with Catherine. At first, he is intrigued by these stories, but the more he listens and records them, the more it becomes a deeper search for an explanation. While Catherine is in her hypnotized state, she speaks of different lifetimes at different points in history. In some of the sessions, Catherine speaks as a "master" soul, answering Weiss's questions about the soul, the Spiritual realm, and deep thoughts about reincarnation.

The story of Catherine has many implications, but one of the most amazing things is that Catherine is healed of her panic attacks. As Weiss takes her into hypnosis, he brings her to points in her life where she experienced a trauma. Through the reviewing of the trauma, she can see that she survives (or her soul survives). This past life regression method becomes one of Weiss's primary tools for helping his patients.

Weiss answers skeptics and critics by explaining that even if you don't believe in past lives, reincarnation or even a soul, the method works. Weiss has helped many patients recover from trauma and difficulties using past life regression.

Through *Many Lives, Many Masters*, Weiss helped me deepen my understanding of my Spirit and my true nature. If my soul survives death, then that makes the end of life much less scary.

After death, I know now that I will continue in my Spiritual form, complete with memories and life lessons. While death may be unknown to me at this point, it is not something I fear.

Can Religion and Woo-woo Co-exist?

I recently read *The Priest and the Medium* by Suzanne Giesemann.[13] It's the true story of how psychic medium B. Anne Gehman and former Jesuit priest Wayne Knoll met, married, and joined their two Spiritual lives together. The author, Ms. Giesemann, is a well-known talented medium herself. She takes great care to explore the childhoods of both Anne and Wayne, how they were brought up, their beliefs about God, and their passions in life. The book is a biography, but the deeper meaning of the book is how we might have different beliefs, traditions, and expressions of our connection to Spirit, but in the end, we have a shared universal Truth that holds it all together.

For me, Giesemann presents a picture of how those from a religious background can approach the woo-woo world and fully participate in woo-woo—learning about psychics, energy healing and the amazing things that woo-woo brings to us!

Religion and woo-woo *can* co-exist. Both affirm and connect with the greater Spirit—God, Source, the Universal Truth. Both affirm love. Both affirm healing.

Religions are the "organized" structures around the Truth which is at the core of our being. Where religion has it right is in those core beliefs of love and healing. Where religion has it wrong is in believing that one religion *owns* the truth whereas other religions are *wrong*.

We're Still Learning

If established religions had their way, all the information we needed about the soul and the Spirit would be from writings dispensed to us 1500 years ago! But our human drive is to learn and explore everything we can. We've explored nearly the entire earth, the moon, the tiny properties of atoms, and we've built systems for communication, food production, transportation, and technological wonders. And I am happy to report that humanity has explored and learned new things about our Spiritual nature. That is woo-woo at its core. The Spiritual explorers are the authors of these wonderful books about energy medicine, divination, near death experiences, mediumship and so many other wonderful subjects.

The point is this—we are still learning about our Spiritual nature, about the "other side," about our true selves. Our knowledge and practice of Spirit do not stand still. There is so much to be learned and explored.

What if you knew the universe was on your side? What if you knew God was not a judgmental God, but was cheering for you, wanting you to succeed? What if you knew God had your back? Just taking that in as truth has the potential to make life easier and more enjoyable, doesn't it?

CHAPTER THREE

....

MODERN CULTURE

I went to a small private university in Michigan and had a group of friends who were all deep thinkers—philosophy and history majors, but also engineers and computer science scholars. I was surrounded by a "thinking" crowd, and I took it for granted that that's how everyone was. Blame it on my good ol' mid-western values.

My good friend Dave moved away to the west coast and when he came back to Michigan to visit, he told me that the one thing he missed most was the deep-thinking conversations. "Everyone over there just wants to talk about their car and their house, and the next car they want to buy and the next house they want to buy," Dave lamented. "It's so boring."

These conversations continued and the more I learned the more I began to see how pervasive materialism had become. I started to wonder: Are we living superficial lives? Is it all about *things?*

Or maybe it's all about *experiences.* The more recent generations have leaned towards rejecting a life of acquiring "stuff" and replaced it with a minimalism centered around experiences. Travel, extreme sports, culinary exploration—all good experiences, but have we simply replaced one kind of obsession with another?

What words describe modern Western culture these days? Thoughtful, peaceful, and affirming? Or anxious, argumentative, and depressed? Clearly, if you watch the news and scroll social media, it's the latter.

Why are we anxious, argumentative, and depressed? For one, I think the fear of the future plays a big part. There is definitely some political fear—what will happen to me if the other side wins the political battle? *I will lose my identity and I will be treated unfairly.*

Another anxiety that people have is fear of loss. What will happen to me if employers and the economy continue in the current direction? *I will lose my source of income, and I will lose my accumulated wealth (however much that might be).*

Finally, relationships make people anxious. Families, marriages, dating and just getting along with neighbors seems to be more difficult lately. The fear of being alone causes anxiety and causes people to make unfortunate choices. *I don't want to be alone.*

Our argumentative nature seems to stem from an attitude that everything must be taken personally. Do you see this, too? How every barb or unkind word needs to be answered and escalated? Every perception of being mistreated needs to be called out and posted? It seems to be the attitude that whatever happens to me is not my fault, and I am justified in my revenge. Not the sort of culture that engenders peace and kindness.

One of my favorite lines from *A Course in Miracles* is

this: "Do you want to be happy, or do you want to be right?"[1] Remembering this has ended hundreds of potential arguments for me.

This might sound familiar—you're in a discussion with your spouse, and you each remember the details of a situation much differently. The more the two of you talk about it, the more different the stories become, and finally you're in a full-blown argument. But really, in 99% of situations, you don't *need* to be right. Your memory of an event is different than that of your spouse's. So what? If you let go of the need to be "right" and decide you'd prefer to be happy, you can let go and end the argument. You might actually *be* right, but you don't need to hold your ground and declare yourself the winner.

This is all connected to the modern culture trap: a mixed bag of cynicism, the "I'm right, you're wrong" mentality, and being "just too busy" to care about joy over power.

Ultimately, it's the refusal or inability to pause and go deeper.

If I Could Just Have...

How often have you heard someone say, "If I could just get that perfect job, everything would be great" or "If I could just find the perfect partner, it would solve everything" or "I just need a bit more money, and I'm all set."

We tend to focus on what we don't have and believe that by filling that void, we will solve our problems and life will be fantastic.

But somehow, our problems follow us to the new job and the new relationship. A bit more money somehow doesn't make us happy either.

When we feel a big part of our lives is missing, or we're in the wrong job or relationship, no wonder we feel sad and anxious.

For some, being anxious or sad is a motivation to find a solution—which was the case for me. It moved me strongly toward wanting to find happiness and the start of my Spiritual journey. For others, however, sadness and anxiety is a downward spiral. If this is you, take hope. There can be another way.

Coping

How do people cope with a life that is anxious and depressed?

(Now, let me step out here for just a moment and say that if you are suffering from deep depression and anxiety, please seek out support from a mental health professional.

A good therapist can work wonders and there are many resources and professionals out there to help.)

When dealing with day-to-day stressors, we all react to our own anxieties in a variety of ways—ways to distract ourselves from the unpleasant feelings we have about our lives.

One distraction is to avoid relationships and connections to other people altogether.

Another way people cope with anxiety and overload is with action—lots of it. You may know a super-busy over-productive work-a-holic family—dad works 80 hours a week at his law firm, mom's a VP in a Fortune 500 firm, and the kids are in every sport and after-school activity. The goal might be financial success, but the hidden result is that there's no time for reflection or depth of Spirit. The idea of asking "why" hasn't crossed their minds or, if it has, it might look something like this:

"Why are you working so much?"
"To make a lot of money."
"Why do you need a lot of money?"
"So that I can have lots of things and experiences."
"Why do you want to have these things and experiences?"
"So that I can enjoy my life."
"Are you enjoying your life?"
"Not really."
"Why not?"
"Because I'm working so much."

This circular logic leaves them back where they started.

And, speaking of money, not everyone is necessarily hungry for it. Those who aren't out to make bazillions of dollars might have found some meaning in life by supporting a cause as another coping strategy. Many of these causes are very important—environmental causes, protecting historical buildings, helping animals, helping veterans, and helping children. Some causes are less altruistic, but still attract lots of energy. For example: politics. In the U.S., politics can be extremely polarizing and often attract the mindset of "the way I see the world is the right way and must be protected. The other side is destroying the world and must be stopped." As the antagonism between the sides increases, the underlying idea of winning at all costs strengthens as well.

Admittedly, I can relate. My college years were spent with deep-thinking friends, but we were also a very cynical bunch. One big barrier to woo-woo, speaking from experience here, is cynicism. At that time, I completely dismissed anything that didn't have a rational explanation or clear logic behind it. My friends and I would laugh at classmates who liked incense and crystals and tease the woo-woo crowd for being illogical. That was part of my journey—needing to be completely steeped in logic before I could reach into my heart. I now look back on that with some shame and sadness.

Cynicism has a deep-seated belief that everyone is acting in their own self-interest, and no one is to be trusted. Politics? Corrupt. Business? Corrupt. Churches? Deluded and corrupt. Psychics? Corrupt scammers. And so on.

As I got into the working world after college, I became less cynical about life. I think what got me on the right path early on was my strong sense of curiosity. I found that you can't be curious about life and also cynical about everything.

Where Does Woo-woo Fit In?

I bring up all of these "modern ills" only to say that woo-woo hasn't connected with everyone yet. The anxious, cynical, or argumentative individual has too much going on in their head (and keeping themselves busy coping) to be able to connect with a deeper purpose; ultimately, woo-woo *is* the expression of a deeper purpose.

If someone is cynical about life, they will be cynical about woo-woo. To them, it may seem like just another cult trying to suck members in and take their money.

If someone is superficially living the busybody life, they likely have no time or inclination to slow down and reflect.

If someone is consumed by a political cause, woo-woo probably doesn't fit in with that "us-versus-them" mentality, and they will likely not have space for it in their life.

What if There's a Better Way?

What if there is a better way? Are we tired of being anxious and argumentative? Is there a way to find some joy amongst all this depressing news around us? What if we could remain in a peaceful state of mind, even when the rest of the world seems to be falling apart?

That's why we're here.

Bring on the woo-woo!

Let me give you a few quick thoughts on finding peace when the rest of the world makes that challenging to do!

One of the first tools I received for staying calm in difficulty was to not respond right away. Take a step back.

Listen. Decide if someone's comment or demand even warrants a response. Don't participate in the argument.

Another tool you have access to right now is meditation. Read on for more discussion on meditation, but for now, know that you can rest your mind, calm the "monkey mind" and feel more joy and peace wherever you are.

If you're interested, perhaps the best way to reach a deeply cynical person is to appeal to their curiosity. If you are curious about a strange fact, you will be interested in finding out more. That curiosity (and being open to the answers) may help open the door to a little more joy and happiness in your life.

Will meditation and curiosity cure all the world's ills? Can you meditate away war, famine, and abuse? Clearly not. But being attuned to Spirit *inside* is the key to surviving what happens *outside*.

Science, Religion and Woo-woo

When I began my woo-woo journey, one of the systems that kept coming into my awareness was Tarot. (More on this later.) I was hesitant to explore Tarot because of the negative opinion of divinatory tools within organized religion.

This fear of learning Tarot was based on a fear that somehow these cards were not good and that they represented the "evils of fortune telling" that the Bible spoke about. If asking God for a sign was frowned upon, then certainly tools of divination were even more forbidden.

It wasn't until I learned that intuition and connecting to Spirit is backed by science *and* is fully part of the human experience, not forbidden by God, that I was fully able to explore the woo-woo that I now embrace.

Science demonstrates that we have the ability to perceive each other through a mysterious connection. Science has shown that we innately have this ability. Science has also shown that those who meditate and connect to this mysterious power can strengthen their ability.

And our modern religions are a combination of universal Truth, tradition, rules, and dogma. By sorting through to find the Truth, and leaving dogma, rules, and tradition behind, we can keep an open mind about this mysterious connection.

And lastly, a part of modern culture tends to scoff at psychic readings, crystals, and healing hands; however, a growing number of modern people are discovering their Spiritual selves and their Spiritual abilities through divination, energy healing and intuition.

How Each System Explains a Setback

Imagine a setback or a disaster that happens to you. For illustrative purposes, let's envision you have just been fired from your job, and the whole situation seems deeply unfair. Put yourself into this situation and truly feel what you might feel—the despair, the sadness, the injustice of it.

Let's see how each system of thinking—modern culture, science, religion and woo-woo—deals with this setback. Here's how four different friends might counsel you on why it happened and what they believe your response should be.

The Message from Modern Culture

Your friend Anna sits you down and has this to say: "This is not your fault. You were wronged! What your company did to you was unfair, and probably illegal. Friend, you need to take stock of the situation, see what's going on, and plan your next move. I know you also need to vent. And if you need to take some revenge, I'm here to tell you that you are justified in your revenge! You need to take some justice into your own hands.

"I know you might just want to walk away—I get that. That could be an appropriate response. But it won't right the wrong—that's up to you. Let's make sure the rest of our friends know how you have been wronged! Let's rally some support! See if I'm right! Ask around! I know we can help you design the perfect measured revenge. Do *not* take this situation lying down! Act boldly. Right the wrong."

The Message from Science

Your friend Tyrone is all about science. Here's what he says: "Go back and figure out what led up to the firing. There are lessons there. Success leaves clues. So does failure. Figure it out. There are details and warning signs. Go back to your own mindset, your thoughts, your assumptions. You might need to work with your therapist on this, right? Go back even further—I bet some of your childhood trauma might still be causing you trouble."

"If you dig deep enough, you'll find the cause, and when you come up with an action plan and make some mental corrections, you'll ensure this doesn't happen again. Let's get you some expert advice, OK? This issue is solvable, but it's up to you to act. The experts know how this stuff works, so think it through thoroughly, and trust what they tell you."

The Message from Judeo-Christianity

Your childhood friend Mara is a deeply religious person, and she knows that your firing is from God. Here's what she says: "You are broken and beaten down, but don't worry; God will forgive you. Somewhere you went astray, and this is God's way of bringing you back. It may feel like a punishment for wrongdoing. It might be. Maybe you were too proud or relying on your own strength.

"God has come to you today to remind you that you need to rely on him alone. I don't mean to be harsh, but I think it's pretty clear that you messed up, and now you are seeing the consequences. This is your wake-up call to return to trust in God. Humble yourself, repent, and see the error of your ways; then return to God, only then will you be restored."

The Message from Woo-woo

Your friend Dawn is centered, giving you peaceful counsel: "Dear friend, you are more capable than you can imagine; Spirit is here to help you do amazing things! Step back and observe your being fired from a distance. I know this might be difficult but see if you can let it go. Let go of the frustration, the anger, the feeling of injustice. Just sit with that pain for a minute, feel into that pain. And then let it go.

"There is a lesson in what happened. Treat this moment as if you had planned it. What would you have wanted to learn from it? Maybe Spirit needed you to move on to begin the next phase of your life. There is so much more in store for you, dear friend!

"Seek to acknowledge the lesson, and then let everything else go. *Now* is what is. The past is past. The future is a thought. Make now truly count.

"Can you feel the joy that Spirit is sending you? You are so very loved! Feel the love that Spirit is wrapping you up with. In this difficult situation, *just be*. Don't do.

"And when you are ready, give love and receive love to those around you. Let the Spirit inside you show you your divinity and guide your being."

The four responses demonstrate various levels of our soul's journey. At the foundation level is anger and revenge. In the science and intellectual level there is thinking, figuring, and trying to logically calculate a solution. In the Judeo-Christian level, there is judgment and obedience to an external truth. And in the woo-woo level, there is being, joy and love.

We will continue to explore all three viewpoints as we advance on our journey together.

What Spirit Says

I recently saw the movie *Kardec* which tells the story of a French educator, Rivail.[2] Rivail is, initially, a complete skeptic about communicating with Spirits; later he discovers that this type of communication may in fact be possible. He sets out to gather proof that mediumship is real. He does so by meeting with several psychic mediums and asking them all the same list of questions. He compiles a book of their channeled answers, finding complete agreement in their responses. This launches him into the position of expert and founder of the Spiritualist movement. He assumes the pseudonym Kardec in his writings.

A couple days after I saw the film, I had a dream in which I was asked to do the same thing: contact a few people who were Spiritually in tune with the other side, ask them some questions and record their answers.

I did exactly that. I asked three psychics who are deeply in touch with Spirit to ask Spirit what advice they would have for us, for the new student of woo-woo. Each of the three psychics spent time communing with Spirit and asking them questions. They will join us at the end of the three parts of our journey together to provide their insights.

Meet Our Psychics

Angie is an energy practitioner and psychic; I met Angie in one of the classes I was taking on Tarot, and we became good friends. Angie is a tell-it-like-it-is kind of person, feisty and full of energy. She channels several Spirit guides, one of them calls himself Matthew.

Reverend J is also a dear friend I met through a course I took. She is a psychic who has also been doing energy healing and energy work for many years. She channels a collective of Spirit guides who refer to themselves as

PESHMA. Rev J and PESHMA provide deep insight and detailed explanations in the channeling sessions.

Shelly is a talented psychic and energy healer, using elements of reiki, light therapy, sound therapy and many other modalities. She is former owner of a woo-woo store in northern Michigan which sold books and products for the spiritual enthusiast, as well as offered classes, tours and readings for her clients.

In this section, I asked questions about what science and religion can learn about Spirit, and what *we* can do, as students of Spirit, when it comes to the objections rooted in science, religion and modern culture. Some of the responses have been edited for brevity or reader comprehension, but otherwise remain as direct verbiage from the channeling.

Angie
Channeling Spirit Guides, Including Matthew

Q. What does science get wrong about our minds, Spirits or souls?

A. The main thing that science gets wrong is the assumption that "If you cannot see it or quantify it, it isn't so." But you can also see the beautiful awakening science is beginning to have where they are actually finding ways to support the effect of the ethereal on the human experience.

Q. Where the scientific community tends to either discount, ignore or speak out against the whole concept of soul and Spirit, should we help the scientific community along or let them be?

A. We have put in place the ones who will influence the scientific community; they are entering the community with more open minds, clarity of thought, and brain balance that allows them to create conversation with the more close-minded in a way that begins to tip the needle toward acceptance. This is a new state of being that must be arrived at organically, a natural process that is already beginning. You see it now in the crystal world and in the opening of the medicine men to begin to embrace working with energy as a way of healing.

Q. For many years, established religion has resisted the idea of connection to Spirit for the average person. What does established religion get wrong about our Spirits and souls?

A. They have everything backwards. Established religion has been getting it wrong for millennia. This is because the establishment is ego-driven, not soul-driven. So much of the structure of religion is created by human egos, and not from the channeled information that could have been accessed. It is a natural human state to fear what cannot be seen. There is no vengeful God, there is no hellfire and damnation. There are no troubled souls, only troubled humans. We suppose the biggest misnomer is the idea of acting in a way that assures arriving at "Heaven" after death. Souls prepare for incarnation while in the ethers. Humans will arrive in the ethers when their physical body expires.

Q. Should we help encourage established religions to see things anew or let them be?

A. Let them be. Look into the statistics that your scientists love so much, and you will see that the people are making that change for themselves. As more and more remember who they are, at the level they can connect, you will find that the oppression of organized religion is losing its stranglehold.

Q. How can we help our tired, frustrated, agitated modern brothers and sisters to see their true Spiritual selves?

A. Walk in the light. You spread the light by simply walking in it. You lead by example. You share your story, but you meet people where they are. One must always be aware of shining the light and casting a spotlight. If you cast a spotlight on an individual or perhaps even a group, you will find they turn and run. They will learn nothing from this exchange. You must allow others to come to you when they are ready. Make yourself a beacon in the dark, they will seek you out naturally. They will come to you when they are ready.

Rev J and PESHMA

Q. What does science get wrong about our minds and Spirit and souls?

A. The first thing that comes up is a very easy answer, and that is the ego. That humanness that comes in. That mindful separation that comes in. Of course, there are scientific things that go on in the human experience where we would not be understood without science, understanding frequency and sound and vibration. And so science has a place in bringing the foundation of understanding to a physicality, and where the disconnect may be is when one who is very scientific does not have their heart open. They are "3D," they are grounded in the human physical form to not be able to see past that.

Q. Should we help the scientific community along by trying to encourage research into Spirit and soul or should we let them be and let them catch up on their own?

A. Well, that is kind of the same thing that is going on on your Earth plane today with folks who are so grounded in "3D" and unable to, not willing to, or not ready to step into an understanding about science and Spirituality.

There is no separation. It's all an illusion of separation.

One of the ways that these walls of set ways break down is the scientific disagreements of "there's *no* proof" or "there *is* proof." It is having that contrast because without contrast you are unable to see where you're going. It's like the rubber band effect going into increasing contrast or tension, saying "Oh no," but it gets to a point where either you stay there or if you let go, then you get propelled forward into seeing things differently.

And part of science is fear-based. For a scientist or one who is very scientifically wired, it can be very fearful to step out of that which is known, the physical world that is scientifically proven. Being in the element of Spirituality, being connected to your higher self can be a scary thing; there is no control, as there is in science. In science, there are controls, there are control groups. There is the idea that if it fits into this scientific box, then it is controlled and if not it's out of control. So, there is an element of fear we feel for some and so some may grasp on to the scientific evidence because it is written, it is proven; to go outside of that can be uncomfortable. It requires that you trust that which you cannot see.

Q. What does established religion get wrong about our Spirits and souls?

A. We feel, again, that a lot of this is a control issue. And to be able to have what is known, as opposed to having trust and faith in something greater than yourself or outside of yourself, which is really *inside* of oneself, because again, there's the illusion of separation.

There are some religions that have beliefs in certain things like reincarnation or past lives and those were taken out or dropped out or phased out because their followers or parishioners are like, "Well, we can do whatever we want, we're coming back anyways." So, it was a way of bringing them back and having that control. Now, do not get us wrong, there is a time, place and space for religion. It is an important part of your earthly experience; however, in the times to come, as one starts to awaken, they'll come into their awareness and ascend; religion will be a thing that is not as doctrine and not as separated in the future as people come into understanding that they are a part of the universe, that there is no separation.

I am You, You are Me, We are We. And that love is the universal religion. And so again, time and space, we cannot say when this will actually come about, but you will see on your earth plane that there will not be as much separation in religions and Spirituality. That is something of the future that will be beautiful.

Q. Should we encourage our established religion practitioners to see things anew or let them come to this on their own?

A. Well, the fascinating thing about religions is that every sector of religion has some aspect of Spirituality connected to it. However, they may not use those words because those are 'woo-woo' words. And every religion, when you think about it, when you go to a service, there is always a time and space for prayer, meditation, so it's just called different things. But each and every religion actually has a Spiritual aspect to it. It's just not stated that way.

Shelly

Q. The first thing I want to ask is do we want to help science along? Do we want to show that there are experiments that show that telepathy works? Is that helpful?

A. I think we're shifting in that direction anyway. The thing is, if a person needs science to prove something, they're probably not ready to wake up anyway, right?

For example, some people don't believe in ghosts. You could drop a ghost in front of them, and they wouldn't believe it. They would chalk it up as, "Oh, I must be having an illusion." So, I don't think you have to use science to prove something, although it's nice to see the science behind it.

And for those of us who are interested in that sort of thing, it's interesting, but not required. A lot of us don't even need to know the science behind it because it's in our hearts, right? We know it intuitively. We don't need to have anything proven to us. But if you're like me, from the "Show

53

Me State," sometimes I want to know why something is, and it just makes more sense.

Another example: Tell me *why* I need to do something, then I'll do it. You know what I mean? You hear that we should meditate. Everybody says, meditate, meditate, meditate. Well, what does that mean? Why should I meditate? But we dig into that and find that it's because it helps you receive more messages and clearer messages. It helps heal you. It helps release fears. These are the reasons why I should be meditating. Not just "Go meditate." That means nothing, unless you know why, right?

Q. Another question is how established religion—pick any established religion—how they tend to oppose the metaphysical, even though all religion has some element of truth, and all religions teach you to connect to God. When it comes to talking about the metaphysical and mediumship and psychics, there's a huge taboo with that sort of thing. And I'm wondering what Spirit has to say about that.

A. The churches have always been known to suppress information; churches teach fear. They teach that you need to look outside yourself to find God. That what you need is outside yourself. And that's simply not true. And that's where all religion fails. They teach people to be in fear of God, that if you don't do these things, you're going to go to hell. And it disempowers people. The church is run by the elites, and their whole thing is to control people, it's control. And you do that by causing fear. And so, you teach people that if they don't follow the rules, they're going to go to hell. That also teaches them not to be critical thinkers. *We'll tell you what to think and believe, and you'll be okay. If you follow us, you'll be okay.* And then that way, we're always looking for solutions outside of ourselves when that's simply not true. Everything we need is inside of ourselves—including medicine. We heal ourselves.

In reality, God is within all of us. And not only is God within all of us, we *are* God. So why do we need a church unless we want to go for social reasons?

Q. Most people that come into the metaphysical have some history in established religion, and I'm wondering if there's a good bridge? Is there something that we can help them along in that process? Or, again, should we let it happen naturally?

A. Well, I think people will seek their answers, and the universe brings to them the path in which to do that. I believe that some people will say "I'm going to go on a [Spiritual] path because the world has changed from the past." Then there are some people who go along a "religious" route, along with their Spiritualism.

But I think as time moves along, you're going to find that all religions dissipate because they're no longer relevant. So, I don't believe that moving forward, religion as we know it today will exist. At least not in the fifth dimension.

Q. It sometimes feels there are a lot of tired, angry, frustrated, jittery people out there. So, what do you see as the best way that light workers can kind of help bring them into the fold? What's our role?

A. Well, we're breaking into different dimensions, and so a lot of the angry people, as the vibrations change, create a bigger amount of noise. And so, I think that we just have to rise above it. And it sounds so cliche. Is that the word? I think so, but it's going to get to the point where we feel solid enough *inside* that that doesn't affect us. That we no longer are at the vibratory level of that [noise]. I think it's just a natural shift that happens to those who are ready to awaken or are awake.

I think it will kind of take care of itself.

This is natural. Everything happening is natural. You don't have to try so hard. That's the bigger issue: people are trying so hard, right? If I don't do this and if I don't do that. Well, I don't think that's really the case. You can't pass into the fifth dimension if you are still carrying a lot of heavy thoughts and heavy emotions and you still have things to heal. That [worry] is just locking us into that third dimension and fighting against nature rather than just letting nature take its course and letting us move through; we're still clinging a bit to that.

When I received the messages that Angie, Shelly and Rev. J had channeled, I was surprised and amazed to see common themes—themes which my own reflection had been emphasizing from the beginning. First, science is not always aligned with our Spiritual selves, but we are making some progress, especially as some scientists are making this their focus and life's work. Secondly, established religion, often focused on control, doesn't allow for individual Spiritual revelation, though some pioneers are pointing in that direction. And lastly, our culture doesn't necessarily appreciate Spiritual practices; however, as Spiritual travelers, we can continue to lead to show there is a better way.

Continue your woo-woo journey with book additions, resource guides and a workbook at www.woowoobook.com.

INTERLUDE
· · · · · · · ·

CHAPTER FOUR

FIVE CORE PRINCIPLES TO FINDING HAPPINESS

At the beginning of this book, I wrote about my search for happiness and finding—instead—a very dark time of death and loss, of sadness and despair, of frustration and anxiety. Even before that dark time in my life, I was anxious about many things. I worked many long hours in my job to "get ahead"—something I believed would lead to more joy. I feared my own future; I feared what would happen if I lost my job or couldn't meet the expectations of my boss, I feared for the future of my interpersonal relationships, and I feared the political future, with much turmoil around me. Needless to say, I was generally fearful.

It's hard to be happy when one is afraid, so clearly I was unhappy as well. I even questioned if I had a right to be happy. I found religion to be empty and not answering the real questions of life. I found science to be logical but smug, pretending to know all the answers and covering up when it fell short. Politics and news were annoying and making my blood boil at every jab from the other side.

In short, I was living in that world of empty religion, science, and modern culture.

No one wishes for disasters or dark days for themselves, but it is *because* of that most difficult time that I was set on my Spiritual journey. The experience of loss was a wakeup call, making those questions of happiness urgent and concrete.

As I began to unravel the very basis of my previous existence, many things came more clearly into focus. Over time, I discovered five core principles that became the foundation for my new woo-woo way of life. Many of these principles are well known, especially if you are already farther along your Spiritual path. But, like everyone else, I needed to learn them one by one.

Core Principle 1: Know where happiness is (and isn't).

I couldn't articulate it at the time, but my search for happiness led me to a truth that has been the most profound thing I have learned. And that is this: Happiness comes from the inside, not from external things, people, or events.

When you read that happiness comes from the inside, you'll either know this deeply and profoundly, or you will feel it is just a cliché. What does this really mean?

Let me talk to the *cliché* perspective for a minute and see if I can make it make sense. Many of us strive for a good life by bringing something seemingly good into our lives—the proverbial great job, happy marriage, beautiful house and even the deeper experiences of travel, finding your purpose, and saving some part of the world.

But these are all external things. And they are all

temporary. What happens when the job that made you happy goes away, or the marriage sours, or the money disappears? *I was happy because I had the job. Now the job is gone, and now I am not happy.*

What if you didn't need anything external to make you happy? Maybe the best way to illustrate this is to take an example that's not a Worst-Case Scenario. Let's say you had an outing planned for the day that included a hike, an outdoor picnic, and a ballgame. But now it's clear that it's going to rain all day. There are a couple ways to deal with this. One is to express frustration and maybe anger that the day's plans have been ruined. And the other is to accept the situation and do something else.

I'm sure you know both kinds of people—the complainer who seems to find difficulty and unpleasantness in almost every situation. And the even-tempered friend who just isn't fazed by anything, no matter how dire.

The first level of this happiness from within is an acceptance of life's circumstances. Could you get to a point where a wrinkle in the day's plans didn't faze you? Could you get to a point where you could accept *what is* and not be upset? I think it's easy to see how that could be possible.

So, then it's just a matter of degree. Accepting what life throws at you when it's small is just the first step. Can you see how someone could accept a larger difficult situation? How about a speeding ticket? A skiing accident? A lost friendship? Those might be a stretch. But it's ultimately a matter of degree. And practice.

The next level of happiness from within is then not only accepting what is, but being happy, *despite* what is.

Another way to think about it is this: if you can let go of

needing something, it is a lot easier to stay on the bright side. By that I mean, if you *need* to go to the hike, picnic, and ball game, and you cannot, because of rain, then you will be unhappy. But if you let go of that need, it becomes easier.

It's simple to see this with a small example, and harder if the disaster is a disease, for example, and you're being asked to let go of the *need* for health. I know.

But, again, it's a matter of degree. If happiness is not dependent on external circumstances, then when the rain comes instead of sun, your mood is not affected. And if you were able to practice this life view, you could get to the point where any external circumstance would not affect your mood.

My biggest woo-woo life lesson was exactly that.

My happiness did not *have to* be dependent on external things.

Wow.

Core Principle 2: Treat each moment as if you had chosen it.

Mind-blowing concept number two is this: Treat each moment as if you had chosen it. I don't remember the very first time I heard this, but I do recall being absolutely stunned by this powerful concept. Part of this life lesson is the idea that each situation you find yourself in is a lesson to be learned. But it goes deeper.

Imagine being in a crisis—a devastating medical diagnosis, a huge financial loss, or the end of a relationship. Amid your anguish and grief, you are asking "Why me? Why this loss?" Then, imagine the peace that comes over you when you realize this is a life lesson and you are only here to learn. What is the lesson in this difficult situation for me? What can I learn from it? Asking that question gets you up and above your situation, and lets you ponder the bigger picture.

Before I get too far into this concept, I want to say that this explanation sometimes feels trite and is often used in church circles as an attempt to help someone going through a difficult time. I remember when I was young and witnessing someone else's loss or difficulty, people at church would say, "Well, God has a plan; we just don't know it." Or "God's ways are wiser than our ways." Those may be true statements, but for someone going through deep difficulties, they may ring hollow and are not always comforting.

Personally, when I went through difficult times, had I known that there was a lesson there for me, I might have found the strength to get through those situations.

Here's where the mind-blowing concept gets deeper: when experiencing a difficult situation, ask yourself the question: what if I had *chosen* this situation? Not only is it a life lesson, but it's a lesson *I had planned to learn?*

Why would I have done that—or what lesson was I wanting to learn so intently that I chose to be in this situation?

In 2015 when I suffered that huge financial loss wiping out half of my income in one incident, I might have gotten through it better with the understanding that I was there for a reason—a lesson needed to be learned.

If I had chosen this situation, why would I have done so? What lesson would there be for me? On the surface, there's a business lesson or two. I needed to do more to diversify my clients, build stronger relationships, and prepare for the hard times.

But even more importantly, the lesson was that I needed to rely on Spirit for my wellbeing, that our best efforts might seem to fail in this physical world, but that my true value hadn't diminished. That the measure of my worth isn't in my income or number of satisfied clients, that Spirit had my back and that I wasn't going to be left with no support. That by relying on Spirit for direction, and utilizing the tools and resources I share throughout this book, I was actually—and surprisingly—strengthened by this loss.

You can take the idea of having planned the life lesson metaphorically if you want. Even that is powerful in a crisis: "Wow, if I had chosen this situation, I would have known there to be a life lesson in here. What is it?"

Each moment—especially difficult ones—contains one such lesson. If you had planned this situation, what would you have planned to learn?

Everything Is as It Should Be

Earlier this year, my family and I attended a conference. My wife and I were talking with the conference organizer, Sandy. A few seconds into the conversation, Sandy pointed to the prayer bead bracelet that I wear and said, "Oh, I like your bracelet. Where did you get it?" I described where I got it and the story behind it, which holds deep meaning for me on my Spiritual path. Sandy simply smiled and nodded in a knowing way.

Later that evening, during the conference closing, one of Sandy's staff members explained how wonderful it was to work with Sandy because she remained calm in every situation. She said that Sandy's words of "Everything is as it should be" were the most helpful peaceful words she had ever taken to heart. And then I realized that Sandy was a kindred soul. Her compliment about my bracelet, her calm demeanor, and her own words of "Everything is as it should be" all connected now. Sandy holds the deep belief that everything is as it should be, and she radiates that peace and calmness to her friends, family and staff.

If we think of each moment as something we had planned, then everything is as it should be. It cannot be otherwise. That understanding takes the anxiety out of the moment, and we can take a breath, relax a bit, and then make good decisions from the point of knowing we are in a good place.

The phrase "Everything is as it should be" isn't without controversy, however. It is possibly the one sentiment that causes more arguments than any other woo-woo phrase. The argument is always something like, "How can you say things are as they should be? We have wars, poverty, and grave illnesses and injustice, and these problems are getting worse! Things are *not* as they should be!"

The concept is the same as loving what is. While I don't condone war or injustice, I accept them as how things are. Paraphrasing Byron Katie, "They are until they aren't," which is her way of saying that things are how they are, and things will change when they are ready to change.[1]

Does that mean we don't work for justice, campaign against intolerance or work for peace? Of course not. But we come to our work for justice not with a rage against the current situation, but with an understanding of how things are, and that we will work diligently to make life better here.

These words go deeper. Everything is as it should be because there is a plan, a divine force behind our actions, a series of events that brought you here right now. *For you*, everything has led to this moment right now. You are here because you are supposed to be here. This, too, is a moment you have chosen to take place.

God Is on Your Side

The idea that "Everything is as it should be" is comforting, but the underlying message is also that God is on your side. The Universe has your back.

If your understanding of God is all about judgment, then these concepts are much harder to accept. But if you see God as being on your side and loving you unconditionally, then knowing that everything is as it should be is supportive, blessing you every step of the way.

As I mentioned in previous chapters about judgment, we could do well to leave behind judgment of others, judgment of ourselves, and the idea that God is wrathful and judgmental.

Anita Moorjani says in *Dying to be Me*, "Unconditional Love is our birthright, not judgment or condemnation, and there's nothing we need to do to earn it. This is simply who and what we are."[2]

I love that. Our birthright is unconditional love. Elsewhere, she says, "Judgment is a 'here' thing, not a 'there' thing." Judgment, condemnation, and revenge are part of our human life, not a part of the Spirit life beyond. If we can remember that, then it's so much easier to accept what life sends our way, seeing difficult moments as lessons to be learned, and that we are here, right now, for a purpose, with the Universe holding us in unconditional love.

Wow! With that, I can truly love all of life!

Core Principle 3: You are not your thoughts. You are the observer.

In learning to practice mindfulness, one of the phrases that comes up from many teachers is that you are not your thoughts. What does that mean in practice? It means that you don't have to believe everything you think. You don't have to go along with every emotion that goes through your mind. You can step back and let that thought or emotion go.

When I discovered this core principle, I felt like I had been given my freedom from a lifelong prison of frustration and unhappiness. "What?! Really? I don't have to believe my own thoughts?! Why didn't anyone tell me this!"

Seriously, the idea that not every thought that goes through your head is worth paying attention to—that was a revelation to me.

The "how" of this takes a little bit of practice, but it's not hard. The image that is often used is that of a river, with leaves floating down the river. Each leaf is a thought. The thoughts come into your awareness, and you watch them pass by you, carried away by the river, and then they are no longer in your awareness.

But who is the "you" watching the river? That is the observer, your consciousness, the part of you that can take a step back and watch from a distance.

This takes some time to cultivate. Most often, especially with strong emotions, we feel them—we *are* those emotions. Anger takes over and we respond harshly. Or fear takes over, and we react. But when we can step back and observe the emotion, we can let it go by like the leaves in the river and not participate in it.

"Let it go, let it go…" How many times have we heard that song, and then done exactly the opposite in our next discussion with a spouse or co-worker? If we can truly "let it go" then we can see the emotion that is coming up, perhaps experience the emotion briefly, and then let that emotion pass.

A few months ago, my mother and I were not getting along. She believed a certain narrative and, for her, that story was truer than the actual truth. She confronted me unexpectedly at my office one morning, and I began to experience the emotions of anger and fear. For a few minutes, I was the observer, watching my angry emotions swell, allowing those emotions to appear and pass by. I was able to respond calmly. And then she said something that triggered me, and in a split second, I *was* the anger. I yelled back, I responded harshly. I knew immediately that I had grabbed onto the anger emotion and ceased to be the observer.

With that one experience, I realized how very hard it is to remain the observer in the heat of the moment. In such moments, we do the best we can. When the moment has passed, we reflect and become the observer again.

What you work on is to allow yourself to be the observer of your life. You're not stuck in it, swimming in a sea of daily unpredictable mini disasters. You're the observer, simply watching from above, able to see yourself and know that you've got this. You let go of the need for snarky responses, put-downs, and judgment. You let go of the need to be *right*. You observe your life from a small distance and are able to just let unpleasant emotions go by.

Self-Talk

In a later chapter, we'll go deeply into the topic of self-talk; however, the concept is directly connected to this idea of watching yourself and observing your own thoughts, so I want to note it briefly here. Self-talk is essentially what it sounds like; it's that conversation you have in your head about yourself. If you are like most people, the conversation doesn't quiet down, and is most often quite critical. Are you your own worst critic? Besides the practice of mindfulness and meditation, there are good techniques to quiet that critical voice in your head. By actively turning around that conversation, you can move your thoughts in a positive direction.

This is good news for another reason. By changing that internal conversation—by becoming less critical of yourself—you automatically start changing how you treat others.

So, working on self-talk is the other part of not giving attention to every thought that goes through your head. Part of the process is just observing and knowing that you are the observer. And the other part of the process is retraining your thoughts to move away from the critical. Taken together, you free your mind immensely.

Core Principle 4: Now is what truly is. Only the present is real.

This core principle helps those fearing the future, or regretting things of the past.

I love this concept because it is very freeing. If I ask you "Where is the future?" you might eventually conclude "It hasn't happened yet, so I guess it's all in my mind."

And if I ask, "Where is the past?" you might reflect and say that it's in the history books and yesterday's newspaper. "But where *is* the past?" I might probe further. And you would concede that it too is in the mind.

So, that leaves the present. Only the present is real. Everything else is just in our minds.

Why is this freeing? Because your fears about an imagined future are unfounded. They haven't come to be. You can let them go. And your regrets about the past—also in the mind—are unnecessary. Let them go, too. Experience the one and only present moment.

And then the next one.

And the next one.

Tomorrow Will Be Better

At the beginning of my woo-woo journey, I was introduced to a Tony Robbins course on DVD. Nowadays Tony Robbins is essentially a household name but, back then, I hadn't even heard of him. I was amazed at how he was able to capture my human basic needs concisely and turn them into a plan for improving my life—thinking better, acting better, and being better.

I felt motivated to follow the methods of the course because it would make my life better—in the future. Somehow, it wasn't so great in the present, but if I could work toward being better, sometime in the future life *would be* better. This is no reflection on Tony Robbins. It reflected my own mindset at the time of *doing* now in order to have a better tomorrow.

I realize now that a good portion of my life was structured around thinking that tomorrow would be better. Today wasn't good, but tomorrow would be better, and all I needed to do was to get to some point in the future, and all would be well.

I studied hard in school and was very good at delayed gratification. Study now and receive the benefits of good grades and a good education in the future. Force myself to practice piano diligently now, to receive the benefits of being a good musician in the future. That's really how building any skill works. You need to put in the time now to receive the benefits later.

Every day, I would push through the unpleasant of today, in order to possibly enjoy some unknown future.

Where that falls apart is if you are *only* just getting through the unpleasant today, and *only* expect to have all your joy in the imagined future. You lose twice. The first loss is that you've given up today. It doesn't count—it's a means to an end, and you probably detest it. The second loss is that the imagined joyous future never arrives. You are constantly in the "tomorrow will be better" mode until the day you die.

For a long time, that is how every day was—every day was unpleasant, and the better future never arrived. I was actually wasting every present day.

When you live this way, you live with the mindset that where you currently are is unpleasant, and you just need to put up with it, because the future will be better. Only the future matters.

I think we can still work toward self-improvement, and we can still do things now that will make life better in the future. Saving for retirement is a good example. You put away some money every month so that in your retirement years, you have enough to live on. But if you view each day with disdain or disappointment, and *only* see the future as what will be enjoyable, you've wasted the present.

With a small mindset change, today is to be enjoyed. Now is the time that is real. Look around, experience where you are right now and feel the joy of right here, right now. Happiness won't come *to* you; it comes *from* you.

Regrets of the Past

The other way people reject the present is by living in the past.

How many times have you heard someone bring up how they were wronged by a parent or a spouse or significant other years and *years* ago, and they are still carrying that pain with them? I recognize that it is very difficult for many of us to just let those hurts go. But stay with me here.

Sometimes this anger and regret can be turned inward. In the 1990's, several of my college friends moved from Michigan to California to take up jobs in the technology world of Silicon Valley. I was invited to go with them. Some of my friends who moved are now millionaires, and I often wonder what it would have been like to be a part of that amazing technology movement and get paid well for working there. For many years, I regretted not going with them and felt I had made one of the biggest mistakes of my life by deciding not to go.

Thankfully, I did not let that decision define me, and was able to move on and work in jobs that were fulfilling.

The true revelation of this happened along my woo-woo journey. I now know that everything is as it should be. I now know there are no wrong paths. Just lessons. If I look back on decisions in life, I see that taking a particular job led to a meeting of that special person, who introduced me to someone else who taught me about something that led me to understand my true nature. Right? Look back on your life and see your path. Each step led to another connection. Each connection brought you to where you would go next.

Can you see how someone might get stuck on the thought that they had missed a big opportunity, living a life of regret over a bad decision?

Where is the past? It's in my mind. What is real? Only the present is real.

One of the tenets of woo-woo is that you are not bound by your past. You can start over each day, fresh and new. Prisons of regret and anger are self-imposed.

Byron Katie's system of "The Work" takes the reader through steps to deal with these regrets and anger.[3]

Much of the anger about the past, both directed at others and at ourselves comes from the "should" of the past. *He should not have done that. I should have made a better choice. People should not behave that way.*

Byron Katie takes us through the process where we say and internalize the obligations that we put on other people—those *are* the problem. By letting go of what I believe other people should and should not do, I am freed from the pain and anger.

She calls this the turn-around. In her process of inquiry, I might start with "My mother made me angry by insulting me in front of others. My mother should not insult me." After the inquiry process, where we end is "My mother *should* insult me in front of others," which is just another way of saying "I release my obligation that my mother must behave in a certain way."

Where is the past? It's in my mind. I am here in the present. This is real. I am OK here. I love what is.

Core Principle 5: Give and receive love.

One of the saddest conclusions that people come to in life is "my life doesn't matter." This sentiment is expressed in different ways but with the same core belief. It may show up as: "what's the point to life?" or "why am I even here?"

While depression has many factors and many causes, one of the factors is the conclusion that what we do doesn't matter.

The mistake in this kind of thinking is the underlying belief that our worth is based on our influence—on doing.

The thinking goes something like this: "I am here to do certain things. If I do them, I will make life better for myself and those around me. I can improve my world by doing."

Then, the realization sets in that even by *doing,* things around me are not getting better. In fact, they are getting worse. Take any example of a relationship crisis, a health crisis, or an economic crisis.

The resounding shout of woo-woo is "Just be! That is enough!"

I admit, when I first heard this, it made no sense at all. *Of course, I can't get ahead by doing nothing and sitting around "being." I'll go broke, and my family will starve.*

But the idea of *just be* contrasts with the fear that we're not doing enough—the fear that no matter how hard we try, it's just not enough effort to make things better.

The universe says, "Dear one, it's not your job to strive and push and stress over doing. Let that go, and just enjoy your presence and being present in life. And when you learn to just *be*, things around you *will become better. Promise!*"

A highlight of my woo-woo journey was finding Marianne Williamson and *A Course in Miracles.* Although Marianne Williamson did not write *A Course in Miracles,* she became its most well-known and passionate champion.

I first heard of Marianne Williamson back in the 1990's. I was on an online forum where Williamson was available for an evening to answer questions via chat. The specific memories have faded, but I remember asking her a question about how to respond when others show unkindness and bigotry. I remember her answer was very helpful to me at the time—you don't respond with words or defensiveness. You respond with love. And it doesn't even need to be verbalized. You just send them love.

I read *A Return to Love: Reflections on the Principles of A Course in Miracles* by Williamson.[4] In this book she explains the basics of the Course and the "miracle" which is this: love is always present in our lives, and the reason we are here is to give and receive love. That concept was so powerful for me. *What do I do when I'm stressed out with too much to do?*

Give and receive love. I feel like I'm not getting anywhere in life. Give and receive love.

The reason we are here is to give and receive love.

It certainly takes the pressure off our "go go go" lifestyle and says, "Just be. Just give and receive love."

My personal recommendation: To really get the most out of the Course, read *Year of Miracles* by Marianne Williamson. She takes the Course and divides up the most powerful passages over a year of readings, so it can be read like a daily meditation.

Being and Doing

A year ago, while I was deep into my woo-woo journey, I accepted a position for my day job working for a dear friend as a technology director. The team had weekly focus times where each staff member was offered the opportunity to provide some soul nourishment—a meditation, a personal story of overcoming difficulty, or a mindfulness exercise.

I was thrilled to be able to talk about my favorite topic of woo-woo within the work context. I spent my designated hour describing how one can get through adversity by accepting and loving what is. Everything is as it should be.

In my years of my journey of woo-woo, this concept has proved more calming and healing than any other concept. *Loving what is* has given me the solid base from which to think and act. I live each day, loving what is—or at least trying to do so!

Unfortunately, I was soon called in to the boss's office and reprimanded for being unproductive and advocating unproductive ideas. She told me "Someone needs to light a fire under your behind and get you motivated to get your work done." Never mind that I was more "productive" working in that role than in any prior job. But to the boss, the idea of "loving what is" boiled down to "accepting mediocrity."

What's the difference? Loving what is means you do not rage against what should not be, but instead accept the circumstances, and proceed from there. You see your circumstances as just that—just circumstances. But you still work toward personal and collective goals, you still seek to work toward justice in the world, and you still live in the world of *doing*.

The difference is that if your whole life revolves around *doing*, then you eventually realize you cannot *do* any more.

But if your life is one of *being* and loving *what is*, you can finally see that your *doing* is part of a bigger whole. *Being* puts you right with Spirit; *doing* is only effective if the *being* is there first.

Only Love Is Real

Let's go deeper into this. I invite you to stay with me here.

In terms of time, the present is the only thing that can be experienced. So, in that sense, only the present is real.

But, as we see in *A Course in Miracles*, there's the "reality" that we experience in the physical world, and then there's the reality of our soul or Spirit. Only one of them is "the real world."

An often-repeated quote is this: "We are not a body that has a soul; we are a soul that has a body." Which part is the real part? I believe it is the soul. The soul or Spirit is eternal, and we are having a temporary human experience.

What is the language or experience of the soul? It is true unbounded joy and love. So, in that sense, says *A Course in Miracles*, only love is real.

In any situation, you can respond in love, or respond in fear. Fear is the response that we have learned in our human experience. Love is the way that our soul would respond. Marianne Williamson in one of her commentaries on the *Course* says, "I think of the mean-Spiritedness of someone, then I affirm that only love is real. I watch a horrible story on the news, then I affirm that only love is real. I feel my fears about this or that, then I affirm that only love is real."

Even though this may sound like denial, in reality it is a perception and a mindset that you are tuned into the Reality of your soul.

In the face of love, fear will melt away.

Ego and Spirit: Two Realities

I read Eckhart Tolle's book *The Power of Now.*[5] Then I read it again. And then I bought the audio book and listened to it. And then I listened to it again. *The Power of Now* is very deep. Tolle tells his own story of being a worrier living a very anxiety-filled life. And then something happened— he found himself almost magically transformed to be at peace. He relays how he reveled in this newfound peace and gradually began to tell others about this peace. *The Power of Now* is the culmination of his teachings about finding peace in life.

Tolle and other authors I love, such as Byron Katie, explain how the past is in our minds, and the future is in our minds, but the present is real. Our minds seem to want to dwell on the past and worry about the future. But to live a peaceful life, we need to let go of those worries of the past and future. Any regrets over past events or anxiety of future events are wasted energy.

Tolle goes on to explain how most pain we feel is due to the resistance to what cannot be changed. When something "bad" happens in life, we suffer twice—the first suffering is the bad thing that happened, and the second suffering is our mental resistance to what happened. "That should not be!" We scream and our anger rages against the injustice of it.

To get rid of the pain, we can act as the observer and view our thoughts from above. And secondly, we stop judging ourselves and others.

One of the most important parts of Tolle's teachings is the concept of the Ego mind and the True Being. The Ego is the part of our minds that wants to be in control, the part that looks back at the past with regret, and the part that makes us anxious about the future. It's that critical voice in our heads. It's the part that judges us for doing that thing poorly and berates us for being too this or too that.

The True Being is that which is underneath. Tolle's exercise that is quite helpful is this: ask yourself, "I wonder what my next thought will be." When you do that, you pause, and you are now observing your own mind. That observer is the True Being. By using that exercise continually, you begin to learn mindfulness, non-judgment and you find a peaceful existence.

Similarly, Deepak Chopra expresses the two-realities concept in *The Spontaneous Fulfillment of Desire*.[6] He calls the two realities the "local domain" and the "non-local domain." In this book, Chopra spends some time describing the physics experiments that prove that our world is not as simple as it appears. (The same physics experiments are also described well in Dean Radin's *Entangled Minds*.) Chopra relates our physical world and our ego as the local domain. The Spiritual side of us is the non-local domain.

But Chopra's main points in this book are more about how we can connect with our non-local domain to fulfill our desires. Chopra talks a lot about *attention* and *intention*. We make an *intention* for something to happen, and we put our *attention* on that good thing, and the universe orchestrates that thing to happen.

Even more interesting is Chopra's discussion about one's own consciousness and the universal consciousness—the idea that all are one. My favorite phrase from Chopra is "I am that, you are that, all this is that. That's all there is."

Eloquently stated. At the level of Spirit, we are all one. Only this physical plane shows us separation.

When the universe is orchestrating to fulfill our desires, coincidences are one of the messages we receive letting us know that things are happening for us. Chopra relates several amazing stories of coincidences in his life. I have experienced numerous inexplicable coincidences, and you likely have as well.

Chopra goes on in *The Spontaneous Fulfillment of Desire* giving us a manual on how to prepare ourselves and foster this non-local domain connection using meditation, mantras, and sutras, seeing ourselves in others, and many other very deep concepts. Each concept has several exercises to go through to practice it and make it part of yourself.

Both Deepak Chopra and Eckhart Tolle take us deep into the concepts of the duality of mind/body and Spirit, of local and non-local domain. Both authors eloquently describe how the "true self" is the Spiritual non-local self, and both give exercises to show how to connect deeply with our true self.

Two World Views

The duality that Deepak Chopra and Eckhart Tolle talk about plays out as two completely different world views.

One way of looking at life is logical and filled with rules, statistics, and best practices. In it, you think and plan and prepare; you calculate how likely you are to get sick, suffer a financial disaster or lose your significant other. You need to protect yourself, not trust strangers, stay safe, and lock your doors. You read crime statistics and plan your route accordingly. You know that it's just a matter of time before you, too, are a victim of, well, whatever it is you are fearfully studying up on. When something does go wrong, you know that the problem was *out there*, caused by an uncaring universe that finally gotcha. And you view every bad news story as confirmation that you are right in your assessment of this unpleasant world.

The other way of looking at life is that the universe has your back. You see a smile from a stranger as a sharing of happiness and joy. You see other human beings as doing the best they can with the consciousness that they have. You celebrate the joys of others as the universe's generosity plays out. And you see your own difficulties and failings as lessons to be learned. Seeing an unpredictable and chaotic world becomes an opportunity to pray more and *be more love* in the world. What is the answer to the world's pain? You know that it is more love, which starts right here, in your own heart. You see that we are all connected, and when one of us has a heart open, filled with love, it lifts us all up to be more loving. That's our purpose here—to give and receive love.

These five core principles continue to ground me in everything I do.

Find where happiness is (and isn't).
Treat each moment as if you had chosen it.
You are not your thoughts.
Only the present is real.
Give and receive love.

Find your foundation, your principles, and let them guide you.

What Spirit Says

It's time to check back in with our Spirit Guides.

Each of our three psychics asked the following questions of Spirit and channeled the answers from the other side. In this section, I asked questions about finding happiness in our lives, and how to stay in the present, letting go of past and future fears.

Angie
Channeling Spirit Guides, Including Matthew

Q. How do we become truly happy in our lives?

A. Happiness is a choice. You must focus on gratitude. Do not dwell on the past or on regret. Choose to embrace joy and not misery. Let go of the attachment to a particular outcome. Find things to do that feed your Soul. Share kindness. Share laughter. Do not engage with the vibrationally mismatched souls who want you to match their vibration. Choose happiness. Attract happiness. Be happiness.

Q. What can we do about past regrets and disappointments?

A. Get over them. Mindfully process those things we regret to understand that the past shapes us into who we are, and who we are right now is perfect. They are an important part of the journey that should be embraced for what they've taught us, but not dwelled upon as if that would change anything. Choose happiness. Not regret.

Q. What can we do about our fears of a disastrous or difficult future?

A. Again, get over them. Some humans are more prone to fears and the idea of disaster. This state of being is the result of a vibrational mismatch between the Soul and the physical body. It may also be the result of what a Soul has chosen to experience in a particular lifetime. If a Soul chooses to experience the energy of wonder in a lifetime, they may actually experience wonder by experiencing the polarity of wonder, or disaster. There is no easy answer here, as the person must be willing to release the fears that are so firmly rooted in their comfort zone. They may need to release family conditioning, vivid imagination, and limiting beliefs. A good first step is to shift focus to the wonder that is present for everyone. It may be varying degrees, but it is always there.

Q. How do we learn to communicate with Spirit?

A. Believe, be quiet, listen, and practice. Everyone must find their own way to connect. The human body, while an amazing feat and miracle, is not always predictable when it comes to this. But if one questions their ability to connect, they almost assuredly will not. When one has an inherent connection to energy, one must also be sure to work on their filter. The place through which the energy is funneled for translation. The ego is an important part of this process, as it translates the energy for the human body to understand.

Q. What are signs from Spirit we can look for?

A. Some of you may find more forcible signs. I like to repeat things. Others like to interact with the physical body in some way. A little trip here, a little knock on the head there…

Many of you see signs in different ways. A sign is us drawing your awareness to something to let you know we are here, we are listening, and we want to share something with you. Signs must be what resonates with you; it may be numbers, and it may be words, symbols, song. You may begin by asking to be shown signs that are easy for you to interpret in the physical world. Pay attention, listen. What is a sign to one of you may not be a sign for another, your own unique experience determines what a sign is. Maybe it's something that reminds you of a loved one who is here with us. Perhaps it is something that reminds you of something you have forgotten. Look for something you see often, then ask us to help you decipher what it means.

Rev J and PESHMA

Q. What can we do about our own past regrets and disappointments and our regrets of the past?

A. This is a beautiful question, as Rev J is going through this. And we always like this saying: "A mistake is never a mistake." If you learn from it, if you make the mistake again, there is still some teaching in that mistake. It is just that: an opportunity to grow and learn.

A lot of times regrets or looking backwards to the past are not remembered in the proper way that things actually happened or because of one's own experiences. It might take it on in a different way, in a lower vibrational way, because that is how they may feel about themselves.

Q. The flip side of that question is what can we do about our fears of a difficult or even disastrous future—looking ahead and fearing the future?

A. Again, that is an aspect of having a disconnect from source and higher self. Because again, "I am You, You are Me, We are We." It's an example of not having a trust in the understanding that everything always works out the way that it is meant to.

When things happen in the present moment or what you may think might be in the future, then it takes you away from connection. It also can have a secondary gain for someone to be that fearful of the future and anxious. But if that person really looks at what actually happened or looks back at similar situations and says, "Now wait a minute, I've gotten through this before."

Now, we do want to say that we do understand that there are things that are definite in the future, and not just building them up in your mind's eye—such as those who are faced with knowing that they are losing a job or that they are losing their house or other material things that are in right front of them. Or for example, a health challenge, a big health challenge that is widespread on the Earth plane, such as the health challenge of cancer. These are very real things, with the very real possibility of imminent dropping of the body—of death and crossing over.

However, it is also in those moments that if you look at those who have chosen to remember their oneness and connect with higher self and Source, their Spirituality or even their Spirit of self can grow and become very, very strong and the human mind and body adapts to that which might be challenging.

This growth can happen when there is a sense of acceptance and a connection, we would go so far to say that. And perhaps the scientific community has proven this or will prove it or has been looking into it—that those who are connected to source, the universe, God as you understand him, will get through the challenging health situation.

And going through that which may seem or appear because everything is fearful.

How an individual is able to get from point A to point B, whether it is through that difficult situation or knowing that they will be dropping their body and crossing over, they are able to more gracefully and comfortably move through those situations than those who are in the lower vibrations, which is the experience of being disconnected from Source self or higher self or source itself.

To be able to move through that in a less fearful way, these situations that are brought upon you, where you see it as fearful, are situations that perhaps are placed in your path to help you to grow, connect and move through.

Shelly

Q. Let's talk about happiness. In a very general way, what is the key to happiness?

A. Realizing that everything you need is inside yourself and you'll have whatever you want once you master that level of energy. And this is very easy, elementary stuff. It's not monetary.

Imagine if we corrected a lot of these problems that society has caused, what would we need all that money for? We wouldn't need to be paying our taxes and giving all our money away. The price of food would be free. There would be economical ways of providing heat to everyone. So, do we even need that in the fifth dimension? What kind of bodies are we going to have? We don't even know what that looks like at this point, so I think it's hard to determine.

But the point is this: Stop trying to look outside yourself. We try to get into love relationships to fill some empty part of ourselves. And I think once you feel whole on the inside, that's the key to happiness.

Q. As people are learning to communicate with Spirit, what would you do or say to encourage someone to learn to communicate with Spirit?

A. Meditate. Meditation is the number one thing. It is always the number one thing. Really. If a person just does that, that's huge in and of itself, and that's really all you need. You can go and practice with other people, get better at doing readings, that sort of thing. But hands down, it is meditation that is the key.

Continue your woo-woo journey with book additions, resource guides and a workbook at www.woowoobook.com.

PART 2
· · · · · · · ·
Woo-Woo in Action: Leveraging Tools and Community

PART 2

···

HOW A WOO-WOO
MIND FEELS

The forthcoming chapters are meant to serve as a menu of tools and practices to provide information about the various components of the woo-woo that I explored—and continue to explore—on my journey. I will share my experiences with each, and my hope is that you explore what might be a fit for you.

Experiment.

Embrace the unknown and unexpected.

Have fun.

Gratitude

My background is Midwestern Christianity. In Christian circles, it is very common to hear people talk about gratitude and being thankful. We thank God in our prayers, and we thank God for this and that circumstance.

Interestingly, I didn't *really* learn gratitude until my Spiritual awakening around age 46.

I see two differences between lip-service gratitude and true gratitude. The first difference is found in what we are grateful for. In the lip-service gratitude of my youth, we could be grateful for good things when they happened, but we would pray that God would take away the unpleasant things that happened. If we received a surprise bonus check in the mail, then *that* we could be thankful for. But if it was a surprise bill, that would be something to pray to God to take away.

Ironically, one of the best verses in the Bible about gratitude and contentment is where St. Paul says, "I have learned in whatever situation I am to be content." If only we had truly practiced that! It feels quite woo-woo in retrospect.

To be sure, it's very difficult to be grateful for unpleasant circumstances. So how do we become content in adversity? Byron Katie's words have been so helpful on this topic. In *Loving What Is*, Katie lays out her Truth about *what is*.[1] Essentially, if you resist what is going on, you suffer twice. First is the initial suffering of the situation, and second is the resistance against your situation. If you can accept your situation, then things get a lot easier because you've eliminated half of the suffering. In fact, the resisting of the situation causes more suffering and longer suffering than the initial situation. Think of the person who was cheated on by a partner, and then spends the rest of their life telling the story about how they were cheated on—suffering each time the story is repeated.

Katie's philosophy is to accept what is—and allow yourself the option to change it. Once you accept what is and even love what is, you are free. Gratitude, then, is truly being grateful for all of life's circumstances.

One other way to look at this is to know that there are no mistakes in life, only lessons. If you can see the lesson in each circumstance and situation, you can be so much more grateful for the lesson than if you view it as being punished or getting a raw deal.

The second way true gratitude is different than lip-service gratitude is the gratitude over the miracles of everyday life. Look out your window or think about the beauty of life around you—sunshine, songbirds, strawberries, little toads hopping through the garden (I just saw one yesterday), a kind word, a compliment from a stranger. It's hard *not* to be grateful for such beauty in our world! If you focus on all the problems in the world, you will feel despair. If you focus on beauty and kindness, you will feel joy. It's all about where you put your attention.

A common recommendation from those on the Spiritual path is to keep a gratitude journal. In their series of books on *The Law of Attraction,* Esther and Jerry Hicks recommend writing a daily journal of things you are grateful for.[2] If you start your day being thankful, you set your day off in the right direction.

These are books written by Esther and Jerry Hicks, but channeled or "downloaded" from something known as *Abraham,* coming from beyond their own minds. In that particular book, Abraham, the channeled author, outlines a process for your morning to start your day.

First, meditate. (More on this later.)

Second, set your intention for the day. This is a process

of seeing your actions you want to take in the day or focusing on a general state of happiness and well-being.

Third, write a gratitude list. Write down 3 to 5 things you are grateful for. This lifts your energy and trains you to focus on the positive things in life—which brings more positive things to you!

Even if things don't feel like they are going well, you can *always* find things to be grateful for. "I am grateful for my good health. I am grateful that I have a comfortable place to sleep. I am grateful I have good food to eat."

In the last few months, by shifting my intention to conscious gratitude, I have become aware of the good things that have been pouring in for me—faster than I ever thought possible! Work opportunities, joyous friendships, connections with kindred souls, warming of relationships— the list goes on and on. I am so grateful!

Kindness and Compassion

"Yes, but is he kind?"

We assess people in many ways, using many characteristics and our own judgment of these characteristics. Kindness is a common one.

Why care about kindness?

I believe kindness goes hand in hand with the Spiritual journey. There might be exceptions, but I have found that those far along their Spiritual path are kind to others, kind to animals, kind to the earth, and kind to themselves. They speak of kindness, and they model kindness.

It makes sense, right? As you leave your ego mind behind, you learn to let go of your petty grievances, you let go of needing to be right, you let go of demands on others, and you let go of how life *should* be. You learn to love what is, and you naturally tend toward kindness.

As a father, I am proud of all of my son's accomplishments in school, sports, art, and other pursuits, but what gives me the most joy is to hear from his teachers that he is kind to others. I believe there is no higher quality than treating others with kindness and respect.

My favorite illustration about kindness and compassion comes from Jack Kornfield's book *Bringing Home the Dharma,* in which he quotes Allan Wallace's illustration of a Tibetan teaching.[3]

Imagine you are leaving the grocery store with arms full of grocery bags, and someone roughly bumps into you knocking you over and sending cans and bags and bottles flying everywhere. You jump up and yell, "What's the matter with you?! Are you blind?!" And then you see that the person who bumped into you actually *is* blind. Your anger immediately melts to compassion, and you say, "I'm sorry. Can I help you up?"

That is our condition. When we realize others are in the same situation or a more difficult situation than we are, we extend to them compassion and kindness. Without a moment of pause, we miss many opportunities. This moment of pause is just one of the gifts that the woo-woo provides to us.

Light, Fun and Playful

As we explore the journey to happiness, it is only natural we might pause to ask: What Does Happiness Look Like?

However, perhaps the first question to ask is actually "What does *un*happiness look like?" That is, what do most people feel most of the time?

If you aren't happy, you'll have thoughts like this: *I'm so bored with life. Nothing seems fun or exciting anymore. I can't stop thinking about the fool I made of myself today. Why do I do such stupid things? Why can't those jerks just leave me alone? Why does my mom keep picking on me? I am doing the best I can. It just never goes right. Everything I do turns to crap. I work so hard at things, and all I get is complaints and criticism. She doesn't care whether I live or die. If she would just back off, life would be a lot easier for everyone, and I would get along with everyone else just fine. He even told me that he likes her more than me. What the hell? I do as much as she does, and this is what I get. We just keep going over the same issues over and over and over and nothing ever gets done, it never gets solved, it never gets any better. Just the same or worse. I just cannot take one more day of this. This is it. I'm done. I'm not even going to try. It's no use, no one cares, and no one even notices.*

Eek. That's harsh. That was me on a rough day, and those thoughts would last for days or weeks, as I slid further into depression, sadness and despair.

What does happiness look like then? Something like this: *That guy just cut me off in traffic. I wonder what's up with that? Maybe a bad day? I'll slow down, let him get ahead. Wow, I have never seen so many trees on this road; I drive this way almost every day and I just noticed the trees. Wow. I'm so thankful for this new day. Now that I've parked, I'm going to close my eyes for a minute to clear my mind; it makes the whole day go better. I want to send D a quick good vibe—just a pleasant thought and an intention of good will. I love the view from here! What an interesting person; her points of view are unusual. Not stressed today—just keeping it all light. This is good. I can see where I'm going and it's all up. I wonder what amazing thing is going to happen to me today?*

Keeping it light, joyful, and fun makes all the difference in the world!

This comes through in *The Teachings of Abraham*—the channeled books by the Abraham collective.[4] In the Abraham books and through many of the recorded sessions of Esther and Jerry, they describe how you can get from the state of depression, anger, and rage to the state of joy and bliss. It's not a one step process.

In the *Abraham* understanding, we can live our best life, and even bring to us the good things we want only when we are in a state of joy and happiness. There's no point in trying to ask for better things to come into our lives when we are grumpy, cynical, or depressed. Like attracts like. This is known as the *Law of Attraction* and has been described in the books and movies called *The Secret.*

Esther and Jerry, through Abraham, describe how "feeling good" is the key to bringing good things into your life. In other words, the state of joy and happiness is the cause of good things, not the result. Most of us have it backwards.

What if (like most people), the state of joy and happiness is not our nature? How do we get there from an emotional state further down the ladder?

Let's say your friend Sarah is despondent. She's given up on life over her partner's behavior, and just can't take it anymore.

You: Tell me how you're doing.

Sarah: I just don't care anymore. He ruined everything, he deeply hurt me, and there's nothing I can even do. I'm completely despondent.

You: Tell me more about how you feel about him.

Sarah: I am just furious with his behavior. I am *so angry* with him! It makes me want to scream!

You: Angry is good. It's a step up from despondent and powerless. What caused you to be so angry?

Sarah: We agreed on a new plan, but he went back to his old behavior the next day. I am so overwhelmed and frustrated with this.

You: Overwhelmed is better and frustrated even better yet. It's another step in the right direction. Do you think you could get to just being pessimistic about it?

Sarah: Yeah, I think I can get there. Things are not going to change. What can I do?

You: Right. How about just boredom?

Sarah: Yeah, I think I can do that. Same old, same old. Not gonna change.

You: How about contentment?

Sarah: Well, that's a stretch now. Contentment…like, "It is what it is?" I might be able to get there.

You: Right! There's hope, right?

Sarah: Yes, I could see how I could get to hopefulness. Hmmm…

The example may be a bit contrived, but you get the point. At each step, Sarah can see how she can get to just one level higher on the emotional scale. She doesn't try to go from despair all the way to joy. She might not even be able to get to that next highest emotion right away. It may take some time. But she simply reaches for the next highest emotion. That's all.

In any difficult situation you find yourself in, see if you can reach for the next higher emotion. No one can jump from rage to joy in one step. Take each step, maybe days or weeks at a time, and see if you can get to just one notch better along the emotional scale. That is the key to reaching joy and happiness.

Let Go of Control

The Indian guru Jiddu Krishnamurti was once giving a speech to his followers and wanted to help them understand how he could be so happy and carefree all the time. He said, "Do you want to know what my secret is? I don't mind what happens."[5]

This led to quite a bit of confusion among his followers

who tried to figure out what he meant, but since then, that idea has become part of the Spiritual traveler's mindset.

Usually I see it written as "I don't mind what happens *to me*." In other words, when good things happen to me, that is wonderful. When bad things happen to me, that is wonderful. My mood or feeling of happiness and joy does not depend on what happens to me or around me. My joy comes from within.

Without this understanding, we spend a huge amount of time and energy trying to keep the good things happening and preventing bad things from happening. We want control. In fact, one of the most stressful kinds of situations is when we think we are in control of a situation, and something happens that we cannot control.

Imagine this paradigm as a lens through which you can view your life's events. You had a job and lost it. Anxiety and stress. You had a relationship, and now it's over. Anxiety. You were healthy, but now you are not. Anxiety. Loss of control.

If you can look at life and say, "I don't mind what happens to me," then things get easier.

I recently read an illustration by psychic medium Suzanne Giesemann about how we can view our own lives.[6] Most of us are familiar with TV dramas, and one of the common techniques TV writers use is the cliff-hanger episode. They keep you wanting to see the next episode, even though you know the show is just a story. In Giesemann's illustration, that is a perfect way to view your life. From the soul's perspective, we know we are in a story. Once I know I'm playing a role, I can enjoy life and my experiences without getting distraught over life's unpleasant cliff-hanger situations. *Will I get over my sickness? Will I get through this financial disaster?* Those are just part of the story, but they do not define me. The real me, my soul, came here to experience life. The idea is that we can observe the parts of our life with the same interest that we do in watching our TV dramas, but not get so caught up in the outcome that it causes suffering.

In their book *The Astonishing Power of Emotions,* Esther and Jerry Hicks illustrate the letting go of control with a wonderful analogy[7]. Imagine you are in a boat on a river. You are rowing upstream, against the current— rowing, rowing, struggling, struggling, and barely inching forward. It's a *lot* of work. That describes us when we try to maintain control or force things to happen the way we want them to.

But then imagine freeing yourself up for a moment, letting the boat turn around, and allowing the current to take you downstream. It's effortless and peaceful. You allow the stream to carry you where it wants to go—where you are meant to go. This is the letting go of control, the trusting that good things will come to you.

The upstream and downstream ideas also tie into the emotional scale mentioned in the previous section.

In *The Astonishing Power of Emotions*, Esther and Jerry Hicks give numerous examples of how someone might be in an "upstream" mode, and how they might approach the same situation in a "downstream" way. In each example, they state how the person having difficulty is expressing their pain and anger. And then through making each statement a little lighter, a little less harsh, they begin to turn the statement around, from an upstream *need to be in control* to a downstream *allowing* for the situation to find its own path.

There are many reasons we might think that paddling upstream is the right way to go. "We've always done it that way." "Hard work is how you succeed." "We are rewarded for our work against the current."

But, in reality, the universe gives you indicators of where you are supposed to go and what you should do to stay in alignment with your true self. Sometimes listening to your emotions, embracing trust, and letting go can lead you to remarkable outcomes.

The book is an amazing deep dive into being in alignment, and how your emotions are that guide to what that alignment looks like.

You Do You

I've mentioned Byron Katie several times already, but I will say again that Byron Katie's work has been a bigger influence on my mindset and my actions than any other thought leader or teacher. Her books and lectures were literally life-changing for me.

One of her deep challenging questions is this: "Whose business is it?" The conversation goes like this.

A follower says to her, "My partner doesn't listen to me and acknowledge me when I talk to him. I feel angry when he doesn't listen." And Katie responds, "Is your partner listening? No. That's the reality of the situation. Whose business is it whom your partner listens to? It's *his* business."

In other words, what is the reality of the situation? What is happening right now? He's not listening. That's the reality.

Whose business is it what he does? His business. To say he *should* act this way or that way is to argue with reality.

Katie says, "When you argue with reality, you lose, but only 100% of the time."

I found that when I no longer *required* other people to act in a certain way, life became much more peaceful and joyful. I pay attention to what I do. You do you. It is complete non-judgment of others.

This is a difficult concept especially when we think about statements like "Everyone should be more kind." While that sounds good, what we're really saying is "If you are not kind, I will judge you" and "I require that other people are more kind."

Katie would say, "Are all people kind? No. That's the reality of the situation. They are unkind until they aren't."

She's not saying that we can't work toward more kindness in the world and show kindness to others. She is saying that when we argue with reality (that people are unkind), we lose. When we argue with reality, we feel stress and pain.

Another way she describes it is this: which of these two is the better way to approach a problem? "I'm angry and frustrated at all the unkindness of others" or "People are unkind. Let me be kind to others and help the world by working on my own unkindness."

If we come at a problem with resistance to what is, we experience stress and anger in our own hearts. But if we accept what is, then we can come at a problem with energy and determination without the stress.

I will work on myself to show kindness and love towards others.

You do you.

Meditation and Mindfulness

I believe meditation is the single most life-changing action that one can take.

There. I said it.

That's a bold statement, but I will make the case for it.

Often in western society, meditation is presented as a "healthy" solution to managing stress. If you have a lot of stress, or suffer from the effects of stress, such as insomnia, high blood pressure, headaches, frequent illness, fatigue, and so on, you can alleviate the stressful symptoms, and even the stress itself, by meditation. Nowadays, you can participate in any of hundreds of meditation groups (both in person and online), use smartphone apps, buy guided meditation recordings, and fully participate in meditation solely for the health benefits. For many, this is all that is needed. A healthy way of managing stress.

But meditation goes deeper. The next "level" of participation in meditation is mindfulness. Whole books have been written on mindfulness but, in brief, mindfulness is living in the moment, being fully present in what is happening right now, and not worrying about regrets of the past or fears of the future. Mindfulness also suggests the idea of the observer, being able to take a step back and observe or witness your own thoughts. Lastly, mindfulness brings with it an element of non-judgment and curiosity. When you can look at your life situation from a perspective outside yourself, life becomes bearable, and even peaceful.

Meditation strengthens mindfulness because in meditation, you need to stay in the present and let your thoughts go by without judgment. The two practices work hand in hand—meditation needs mindfulness, and mindfulness is strengthened by meditation.

In the eastern philosophies and religions, meditation is the key to connecting with the soul. This is its true power and meaning.

How does mindfulness work in the real world? Well, if you look out the window on a rainy day, you might think "What a lousy day." But if you were mindful or aware of yourself, your next thought might be "Hey, who said that?" And your next thought might be "Shhh, I don't need to listen to you right now," combined with a little humor, and maybe a bit of happiness, and then a feeling of peace.

As with Core Principle Three: through this process you realize you are not your thoughts. You're the one observing your thoughts. With that little bit of distance, you realize you don't have to believe everything that comes into your mind. You can choose to let a thought go—just let it go—and whatever might have bothered you in the past is just gone. What a relief! Discontent, unhappiness, frustration—it all just melts away!

An even *deeper* level of mindfulness is when you discover meditation as your connection with the divine. The strongest connection we can make with Spirit occurs when we clear our thoughts, clear our own selves out of the way, set aside the "me" and let Spirit enter in. With a quiet mind, Spirit has space to talk with you. This doesn't happen until you've been doing meditation for a while—it takes time to get to the point where you can stay still and clear long enough. But the deep connection is so totally amazing.

For me, getting into meditation was not automatic, and I resisted the idea of it for a long time—it seemed a little too out there (dare I say, "a little too woo-woo?") and I just felt silly trying it. Eventually, I got comfortable with meditation and found the right time and place—for me—to do it.

For those new to meditation, sometimes the very idea conjures an image of hours spent in the lotus position chanting a mantra and burning incense. Lots of incense. I actually started by sitting on my couch and let my mind completely rest for 20 minutes. That's all meditation is. Clear your mind. Stop the incessant thinking, stop the replaying of that argument in the past, stop the constant worry about the painful conversation you need to have next week. It takes time to get there. But gradually, the more you do it, the longer the space between thoughts, and the less anxiety you have. It works.

Tapping and EFT

The next amazing thing I learned was something I also had difficulty accepting at first. This surprise I learned about was a relatively new technique for clearing up psychological issues called EFT, which stands for Emotional Freedom Technique. Also known as "tapping," it is a technique used to "reprogram" your mind to eliminate self-defeating thoughts. I was very skeptical, but amazed and hopeful about this technique. The books I read about it explained the science behind it, and with good science I was able to trust it was real and would work. Since, at this time, I was at the beginning of my Spiritual journey, having science support something as "far out" as tapping helped me believe that it could be real.

I read *Tapping into Wealth*, by Margaret M Lynch.[8] Tapping sounded "out there," but the author had come from a science and engineering background and explained how it worked. I was willing to give it a try. Using tapping techniques, I was able to reduce and even eliminate painful emotional reactions to past events.

The process starts with you identifying a thought or experience that gives you stress or anxiety. You also rate the intensity of that thought from 0 to 10, with zero being the least intense.

Next you create a setup script or phrase. For example, something like, "Even though I am anxious about not making enough money, I deeply accept myself."

You then state the setup phrase while tapping on one of the energy points, such as the side of the hand.

While repeating a script or phrase that describes the stressful experience, you tap your fingers on the remaining specific energy points or meridians on your body. You could also just repeat the word "feeling anxious" or some other variation of the first part of the script. Each time you repeat the process, the stress response is reduced. The reduction of the stressful or anxiety-producing thought is eventually permanent.

That's it.

Step 1: Identify the thought that gives you stress and rate the intensity.

Step 2: Create your setup script.

Step 3: While repeating the script, tap on the energy points.

It seems impossibly simple, but it really works. I have experienced its power first-hand.

This was a big deal for me because I was able to reduce some of my stress and anxiety. Like the self-talk that I learned, tapping allowed me to inch toward a more happy and joyful life experience.

The bigger change, though, was the understanding and direct experience of how the mind and the body are connected. I learned that I could program and correct both emotional and mental difficulties using EFT. I learned that the body and mind were so intimately connected. This set the stage for me to discover even more amazing truths later.

If I could solve an emotional problem by a physical action, then our minds and bodies must hold some very amazing secrets!

Visualization

Top athletes know that visualizing their performance is as helpful to succeeding as actually practicing. Many Olympic athletes not only visualize the sport or race, but they also visualize the content of the news conference after the event, or the walk up the hill before the event begins. Seeing their perfect performance in their mind's eye *actually helps* performance.

So too with non-athletic endeavors. Esther and Jerry Hicks' *The Law of Attraction* books amazed me again and again showing how the visualization of one's success and feeling the joyful emotions of something before it happens brings it into being.[9] In one of her channeling sessions, Hicks says, "Use your imagination until your big dream feels so familiar that its manifestation is the next logical step."

Have you ever made a vision board? A vision board is a collection of pictures and phrases that a center around what you are trying to manifest or bring into your life. Several years ago, I made a vision board which contained lots of physical things that I wanted to have—physical comfort things. I looked at it every day for many months, and then, as often happens, life got in the way, and it got set aside.

As I grew and my understanding about why I was here became deeper and more complete, my goals in life changed, life became less about physical things and more about relationships and connecting with people.

One day a few years after I had created the vision board, I found it while looking for something else. (Isn't that always the way it happens?) I looked at the ten things on the vision board and was very surprised to find out that six or seven of the things—the house, the car, the vacation home and so on—weren't even of interest to me anymore. And the three or four relationships and connections I had wanted to manifest had already happened. Isn't that interesting? The visualizations had all either come into my reality or were no longer needed or wanted.

One of my favorite passages comes from Deepak Chopra's *The Spontaneous Fulfillment of Desire* where he says: "In the beginning, you can be as selfish as you want. In the beginning, your intentions may be all about the "self" and the little details of what you want to happen in your life. But eventually, you will realize that the goal is fulfillment at all levels, not just the personal or ego level. As you start to see the fulfillment of your intentions, your self-interest will diminish because you know you can have it all. When you have enough to eat, you don't obsess about food all the time. It's the same with intentions. When you know that fulfillment is possible, you will think less about your personal needs and more about the needs of the rest of the world."

Journaling

I'm not a journaler. I'm a writer. I love to write. But I don't keep a diary or a journal going for more than a couple weeks. Life seems to get in the way, and I get so much more out of the other activities such as visualization and meditation. However, I do recognize the power in putting pen to paper to connect deeply with Spirit.

I've come up with a couple of workarounds that seem to make journaling a bit easier to do. One approach is to journal with a specific end in mind. I have done several 21-day challenges and am in the process of beginning a 40-day journaling activity. If I know that I have a specific end date, I can begin. I know it's not *forever*. I can see that I just need to be disciplined to write a daily journal entry for a few weeks.

Journaling on a specific topic is also very powerful. A good practice to start with is a Gratitude Journal. Each journal entry is just a sentence or two of what I am grateful for. Gratitude is a very deep and integral part of Spirituality, and by writing every day what I am grateful for, I begin to see all the blessings and miracles around me.

Affirmations

Affirmations are the daily repeated words that affirm something positive about your life. At the beginning of my journey, I wrote a daily affirmation 21 times, and I held to that practice for many, many months. The key to affirmations is that you can't lie to yourself (or the Universe for that matter). If you repeat an affirmation that isn't believable, it's just words.

An affirmation of something like "I am receiving the $10,000 in new business contracts this month" sounds like an affirmation, but there's so much doubt connected with the time and the amount, that it doesn't really work for me. What if it's not $10k? What if it's next month and not this month?

Going back to gratitude for a moment, I've found that the best affirmations are affirmations of gratitude. "I am grateful for the blessings that I *do already* have." That resonates deeply with me. And "I am grateful for the new blessings that are already on their way to me" also feels light.

Self-Talk Actually Works

As I mentioned before, my woo-woo journey started when my life fell apart. I owned a business at the time and lost a customer that comprised more than half of my income. In a five-minute conversation, I was let go, and I lost the ability to provide for my family. On that same week, my father died of pancreatic cancer.

Prior to that, I had been searching for happiness, wondering why I wasn't happy, and even trying to determine if I was supposed to be happy.

The disaster that became my life now caused me to search for happiness in earnest.

One topic that continued to surface during my search was that of self-talk. After a year of intense suffering, I found *What To Say When You Talk To Yourself* by Shad Helmstetter.[10] This was a turning point in my life, a very big "aha" moment.

Through this book, I gained the realization that much of my messy life and dissatisfaction was because of the conversations in my own head. Through self-talk, I was able to change my attitude and understanding to be better and was happier because of it.

Self-talk is something that almost everyone does. It's the quiet internal narrative that goes through every activity in your life. In response to a failure, it might be something like, "Well, there we go again. Nothing I ever do turns out right." And to good news, the response might be, "Well, something is bound to come along and take this good thing away from me. It's just a matter of when."

Think about the conversations in your own head. If you're like most people, they run constantly. That "person in your head" never shuts up! It's a barrage of constant self-criticism. Or the constant replaying of what went wrong. Or constant worries about how bad things are going to get.

I learned that I could turn that around.

Helmstetter teaches you how to observe your own thoughts. Through the practice of being mindful of my own thoughts I realized I could consciously ask myself "Why did I just think that thought?" If the thought was negative, I could replace it with a positive one. Two life-altering observations came out of this experience.

First, I learned that I could put myself in control of the self-talk and put myself in a positive direction.

Secondly, I learned that I could re-program a self-critical mind to be kind to myself. When I am kind to myself and end the critical voice in my head, I can be kind to others and become happier in the process.

This was the first step in my journey. I recommend learning this practice to anyone struggling with happiness or meaning in their lives.

The Miracle Morning

Things were becoming clearer for me as I learned about self-care and the activities and practices that would bring lasting happiness. Meditation was a part of it, self-talk was a part of it, visualization was a part of it, and I learned there were even more things that would help.

One of the problems to solve in doing all these wonderful practices was time, as our modern culture trap would creep back in. *When could I do them*? I was already busy beyond busy. When on earth would I have time to sit for 20 or 30 minutes to do everything?

While I was learning meditation, I came across *The Miracle Morning* by Hal Elrod.[11] This book was also pivotal. I was trying to learn meditation and affirmations to improve my life and had only made slight progress. This book completely solved the what, the when, and the how.

Hal Elrod's story is amazing, having had a near death experience *twice*. He describes being at rock bottom and not only recovering but thriving and going on to lead an amazing life. He describes how he came up with a system to greatly improve his quality of life and accomplish more.

The Miracle Morning provided a structure and a method to helping me along the path of self-improvement (and ultimately Spiritual development). If you want a bit more structure to your journey, especially at the beginning, learn Elrod's system.

Each morning begins with six activities and Elrod also created an acronym to assist in remembering each part of the morning routine. The six elements are Silence (meditation), Affirmations (self-talk), Visualization, Exercise, Reading and Scribing (his term for journaling). The first letters of these words spell out SAVERS.

The key for me was realizing that I could "get away with" spending five minutes on each one for a half-hour routine. Of course, the more I practiced each skill, the more I wanted to spend more time at it, so it quickly became easier to take an hour in the morning for the routine.

By being consistent with the system each day, I found greater peace of mind, I accomplished more during the day, but most importantly, I found I was generally happier.

Because of the *Miracle Morning*, I began these daily habits, however bumbling it felt at the beginning. Things truly began to change for the better.

CHAPTER SIX

WOO-WOO IS TWO WAY COMMUNICATION

Many people believe in prayer, though we don't ever get an answer back. Mainstream Christianity teaches us that the reading of the Bible is the reliable way to know what God is telling us. Woo-woo, on the other hand, is ultimately about communication with Spirit. It is literally a conversation. I pray—or set my intention—and I receive intuition back from Spirit to know what to do. The deeper we go into woo-woo, the clearer that communication becomes.

Signs from the Universe

During my awakening as I moved deeper along my woo-woo journey, I began to feel the presence of someone or something trying to get my attention. During my meditation I could feel that presence and throughout the day I would be reminded of Spirit—things would pop into my mind that would bring me back to gratitude and knowing that I was taken care of.

Strangely, that presence seemed to want to poke me awake in the middle of the night. For nearly a month I would wake up at night and the time would be 2:34 or 2:43 or 4:32 or 4:23. It was the most uncanny, weird sensation I had ever felt. *What is this wild number thing going on???* I thought there must be some significance to the numbers. I was the oldest of my three siblings, so I thought maybe there was some significance to the fact that I was 1, and my siblings 2, 3 and 4 were in the message. I asked several of my woo-woo mentors and friends and soon came to the realization that these numbers were likely simply a message to pay attention to Spirit. While the numbers do have special meanings in numerology, the message I was being given was *Pay attention! I have more to tell you!* So, I did. I listened, I meditated, and I asked questions. I was not disappointed.

One of my favorite authors of all time is Laura Lynne Jackson, a well-known psychic medium who wrote *The Light Between Us* and *Signs: The Secret Language of the Universe.*[1]

I could literally not put *The Light Between Us* down— the stories of her work as a medium were so amazing, so interesting and the stories so beautifully told; I read that book in one sitting, turning pages deep into the night to finish it.[2]

Jackson describes her abilities to see Spirits at a very young age; this ability runs in her family (which is common with mediums). She shares that she wanted to fit in and have a normal job, but all the while being able to connect with Spiritual beings.

One of the most interesting parts is Jackson's description

of the Forever Family Foundation, a non-profit organization that helps families connect with loved ones from the other side. The Forever Family Foundation (FFF) tests and certifies every medium that wants to work with them. The tests are rigorous and would be impossible to pass if someone were not a medium capable of connecting with Spirits.

Why is this validation important? It refutes the claim by some people that "all mediums are frauds." With proper scientific testing and certification, it's a lot harder to claim that it's trickery and fraud. And if there is good proof that mediumship is real? Wow!

I learned, through Jackson, much more information and background stories of psychics and mediums. Of course, there are charlatans and frauds in that industry, but there are also conscientious vetted expert mediums who are the real deal. Jackson's descriptions of the tests and vetting process were very interesting and enlightening.

Laura Lynn Jackson spends a lot of time in her books describing the ways that Spirit communicates with us. It is different for each person, but there are some common threads. For one person, it's a certain kind of animal or bug that appears frequently, like a dragonfly or butterfly. For another, might be feathers that appear just when she is thinking about needing a sign from the universe on a particular topic.

In my case, I see repeating numbers *all the time*. I might be working hard for several hours on a day-job task, look at the clock on my computer and see 2:22. Then a few minutes later I see a note that my software needs an update to version 3.33. Later in the day, I'll see I have 777 new notifications on a particular message platform. Then in the car, my odometer shows 8888 when start the car.

The repeating numbers are relentless. But it's not like I am bothered by it! These are reminders to stay connected to Spirit! While the actual numbers have some numerology significance, the message for me is that I am reminded that the angels, Spirit, the Universe is on my side. I offer a prayer of gratitude each time I am reminded. It's a wonderful way to remain grateful throughout the day and know that Spirit is right there guiding me.

We each simply need to be open and watching in order to find our signs.

Signs from the Angels

For me, the numbers continued.

A few years ago, over a holiday weekend, our family spent time at a state park in Michigan, right on Lake Huron, one of the Great Lakes.

One of my favorite things to do is to listen to the waves, watch them crash up on the beach, and walk along the beach to just *be*.

At that time, I was very concerned about our finances in general. It was during the pandemic, business was slow, and I was caught between running my business and my dream and desire to work as a healer. Which one could pay the bills, and which one was the true direction I needed to go? And were they the same thing?

As I walked along the beach, I stopped to watch the waves wash up against the sand. Then I looked down and saw a perfect circle in the wet sand next to my feet, indicating something just under the surface of the sand.

I reached down and pulled a quarter out of the sand!

I immediately thought it might be a sign not to worry about money…but then also thought it was probably just a coincidence.

Immediately, after the next wave washed away, another perfect circle showed up in the sand—another quarter!

As I pondered the things I had read about manifesting what we need, I walked further along the beach, and another coin washed in with the next wave!

Now I knew it must be a sign. Thinking about this wonder I got really excited. Here and there, more perfect circles appeared in the wet sand, revealing more coins underneath.

A while later, when it was time to go, I told my wife, half-joking "I'm going to walk down the beach one more time to manifest another quarter; then we can leave."

I walked about ten steps, and then looked down, and there it was. Another quarter.

This was one of the clearest signs of abundance that I had ever received. The Lake was nearly laughing with me, celebrating the joy with me, and whispering to me that I would always have what I needed. I would manifest what I need, and *I would be taken care of.*

I left that lake shore buzzing with excitement about all I had experienced and realized.

But what happened next was even *more* amazing.

Back at our cabin, I was thinking about all this, and was wondering about the strange thing that had just happened, thinking about that assortment of coins that had washed up on the beach. I took the small handful of coins out of my pocket and counted them: four quarters, a dime, and a penny.

That comes to $1.11.

That's 111. In numerology, 111 often represents *the manifesting of thoughts into reality.*

I am warmed by knowing that the Universe sent me a very strong message of money, and the repeating number *and* the numerology meaning of the number. Altogether, the significance of that event is off the charts.

Tarot

But numbers and signs weren't the only things finding me once I opened up.

To paraphrase an old saying, *You don't find Tarot, Tarot finds you.*

I remember looking back to when I was a child and teenager. As I mentioned, Tarot represented something dark and unnatural. I didn't know anyone who read Tarot when

I was young, but I do remember seeing a deck one time and either shrinking away from it, or being told it was not to be touched, and that it wasn't a good thing—all very vague memories, of course, but definitely not positive associations.

So, when I signed up for a book club that sends daily e-book recommendations, I had to pause at *How to Read Tarot* by Jessica Wiggan.[3] The book was offered for $2. Well, I figured there was no harm in simply buying a book about Tarot. I was exploring all the amazing ways I could interact with Spirit, and maybe Tarot would shed some light on that after all.

I read the book straight through, and by the time I was done, I knew I needed to learn more. I was not ready to buy a Tarot deck yet, but I did download a free Tarot app for my phone. I started learning the cards by using the app.

Some strange things happened over the next few weeks. On a vacation to northern Michigan, my family and I were in a coffee shop with an attached gift shop. I kept feeling drawn to one corner of the shop. When I finally went there, I was surprised to see a whole table display of different Tarot decks. I was very curious but did not buy a deck.

Later in the same month, I was in a little gardening store, and again felt drawn to a section of the shop where—again—I saw a table display of Tarot decks.

OK, Spirit, I'm listening. I'll get a deck. Soon.

I finally bought a deck when I passed by a store that had Tarot decks displayed in the front window.

And for the next four months, I read Tarot books and practiced Tarot reading.

What does a Tarot reading look like? If you receive a Tarot reading, the reader will likely ask you, "What is your question?" You might have a specific question about work or a relationship or difficulty you are dealing with. Or you might just want a general reading about what's coming up the next few weeks. The Tarot reader will lay out the cards in a pattern on the table called a "spread." A spread will have between three and ten cards (sometimes more), and the positions of each card are significant. A 3-card spread might have positions of *past, present,* and *future.* Each of the three cards is turned over, and the reader sees which card is in the past spot, the present spot and the future spot.

Here's a quick example without getting into specifics of the cards: you might see a card representing struggle in the past position, learning in the present position, and abundance in the future position. Interpretation: you've been struggling with this issue through your recent past, you are learning new ways of dealing with it, and you will be successful with this, so keep going. You're going in the right direction.

I want to step aside here and answer some potential doubters. I have heard skeptics say (and I used to believe) that dealing random cards to gain insight into one's life was as sensible as flipping a coin to see who to marry. All readers of Tarot and any kind of divination know that it is not the cards that carry the power, it's the person. We are intuitive beings, and those who are willing to listen to our intuition (which is actually listening to the divine), are able to learn much about their own lives, and can help intuit direction for the lives of others who ask. Random cards? No. Cards directed by the divine, and used as a tool to enhance our intuition? Absolutely

The connection to our Spiritual selves and to the greater

Spiritual realm is a *two-way connection*. **Prayer is our communication to the divine. Intuition is the divine connecting back.** I believe that is the most important thing I have learned in this lifetime—listening to my intuition, to the Spirit's messages.

Prior to buying my Tarot deck, I had read *How to Be Your Own Genie* by Radleigh Valentine.[4] I quickly signed up for a course he was teaching online and joined the community Facebook group (more on this later). In one session of Radleigh's Tarot course, he said something very interesting. This was one of the most important things that I learned during the class itself. Radleigh said, "I want to tell you a secret—I don't actually need the cards anymore."

What did he mean by that? That his intuition had been so honed and sharpened that the message that the cards would present actually comes to him *without* the cards. As a beginner Tarot reader, I rely on the cards to lead me toward the message that I am to give to my client (or receive for myself). But as that intuition gets sharpened, the message becomes clearer and comes with more detail than the cards can provide. At some point, the message comes clearly through intuition, and the cards are extra detail.

Tarot is the combination of a picture language and intuition; it's letting Spirit speak through the cards.

Meditation

Here we are back at meditation again. While on my woo-woo journey, I learned that meditation is a core principle—*the* principle, in fact—to finding and living my true self.

In the first part of the book, I described how meditation

can be a method of calming the mind, of clearing out upsetting thoughts, and stopping the "monkey mind" from taking over.

In this section, let's look at meditation again, but as a deep Spiritual practice and as it relates to this two-way communication.

At this stage, you know your true self is the Spirit/soul/non-local part of you. Prayer is us reaching out to Source or Spirit, and intuition is Source reaching back to us and communicating back. Intuition doesn't come naturally for many people; however, it is a skill that can be learned and practiced.

How to hone that skill? Meditation. It takes time to listen and discern what the "voice" of your intuition sounds like.

When I was right in the middle of my Spiritual awakening, I spent time trying to understand the difference between my own thoughts (the "ego" mind) and what might be a message or a voice of intuition. I recall one instance very clearly. I was in the car at a stoplight, waiting to turn left. The stop light gave me the green left-turn arrow, and I was about to make my turn when I heard a "voice" in my head say, "Stop! Don't turn. Someone's going to run the red." A second later, a car came flying up over the little hill and sped through their red light. Had I ignored the voice and turned left, it would have been a serious accident.

That is the voice of intuition—or better to call it the voice of *Spirit*. (Strangely enough, when I try to place the location of that voice in space, it feels like it comes from behind and to the right. The "ego" voice of my own thoughts is in front. Maybe it's just me, or maybe others have had similar experiences.)

The point of this intuition story is that I was able to truly listen only when my own mind was quiet. By quieting the mind, there is space to listen. By listening, you can learn to hear your intuition or *Spirit* speak.

This experience is not unique to the woo-woo crowd. I remember in high school having a conversation with a classmate who went to a different church denomination than I did. She was telling me how the Spirit of God spoke to her and let her know what to do in a certain situation. I remember thinking sarcastically at the time, "Oh, so *God* speaks to *you*, does he?" My stifled intellectual Christian denomination would not allow for that possibility in humans. We were taught that after the Bible was written, God stopped speaking to us.

Now looking back, I realize she was probably *very* in tune with her soul, and hearing Spirit speak was something she had learned by prayer and deep meditation on scripture.

My experiences have given me a new respect for other denominations and religions that speak of hearing messages from God. Clearly, not every word spoken in God's name is true, but those who have made a true Spiritual connection can and do hear the words of Spirit. You can too. Meditation is one way to get there.

Divination, Intuition and Knowing Things

As I studied Tarot and learned more about my intuition, I began to realize there were *many* divination tools available— some very ancient and some just old. While studying a Tarot book, I was made aware of Lenormand; while reading a history of magic, I found out about ancient runes. Like a path of breadcrumbs, each new discovery led to the next. I was very curious and fascinated with these tools and systems, so I explored and learned about each one.

Another favorite author on this topic is Radleigh Valentine, who wrote, among other referenced books, *Compendium of Magical Things.*[5] In this book, Valentine takes a chapter to describe each of the various divination tools, how they work, a bit of the history of each one, and some features that make each one unique. I found a kindred Spirit with Radleigh Valentine in that he was so interested in each system and found each one compelling to learn and use. Valentine has made his name in Tarot and is a very accomplished reader and teacher of Tarot; his deep knowledge of the esoteric world made him uniquely qualified to write a book about the many magical systems available.

The I Ching

In my own life, Tarot has become my focus; however, I spent many months learning dowsing (using a pendulum), ancient runes, and the I Ching.

While in college, I studied Chinese language; after college I lived in Taiwan for five years during the 1990's; I have always been interested in Chinese culture. I am sure there are echoes of a past life in China.

I knew something about the I Ching, but I did not realize it was a complete divination system until I read the book *The Man in the High Castle* by Philip K. Dick.[6] Philip

K. Dick is a science fiction author, having had many of his books turned into well-known movies. *The Man in the High Castle* (also a TV series) is a book about an alternative history in which the Axis won World War II. The main characters use the I Ching to help with decisions and determine their best course of action. That truly piqued my interest when I read it, and I began to study the I Ching.

The I Ching is likely the oldest divination system still in use today. The system consists of three coins which are cast to "build" a six-line hexagram and a book (the *I Ching*) which has an interpretation for each of the 64 hexagrams. Because the writings are so old, and because there have been many commentaries woven into the *I Ching* texts, it is quite difficult to understand in its original form. Most users of the I Ching use a recent translation that attempts to make some modern sense of the ancient poetic texts.

Receiving an I Ching reading is similar to receiving a Tarot reading. As a client, you have a specific question in mind, or a general part of life that you need guidance on—love and relationships, health and wellness, or business and career. The I Ching reading will sound very poetic and sometimes rather obscure. As the client, you will need to interpret the words and images in the context of your question.

I researched a great deal to help me understand the I Ching. One work was by Paul O'Brien called *The Visionary I Ching: A Book of Changes for Intuitive Decision Making.*[7] O'Brien ties in modern concepts and ideas about intuition and softens the I Ching's traditional military imagery for our modern world. I really connected with O'Brien's writing, and it made the I Ching useful as a divination tool.

The other book I really enjoyed is *The Clear-Cut I Ching or The Book of Changes for Beginners, Vol 1*, by Master S. R. Chang.[8] This work feels like a secret document written by an insider who knows how the I Ching *really* works. The author explains how much of western I Ching understanding is done in trying to mull over and decipher the ancient texts, but Chang takes a different approach. He presents short *essence of meaning* texts for each hexagram, so the process feels more like a traditional intuitive oracle card reading.

One thing I really like about the I Ching is the fact that all you need to use it are three coins and a book. No special tools required. I also like that it is very old and has stood the test of time—thousands of years!

Dowsing

Dowsing is the use of a pendulum or other tool to receive an answer to a question. There seem to be two categories of dowsers—old school dowsers using dowsing rods to determine where to dig wells and modern mystics who use a pendulum to ask a question about life.

When I bought my first pendulum, I did not realize that the method of using it was related to the water-finding dowsing crowd. I remember how dowsing, as with many metaphysical explorations, was portrayed on TV as comical and silly. There's a *Gilligan's Island* episode where the island is running out of fresh water, and the Skipper and Gilligan use wooden dowsing rods to find water. Of course, the Professor scoffs at the use of dowsing rods.

So, I was very surprised to learn that dowsing works, that there are professional dowsing organizations, and that the process is taken very seriously. (Those wooden Y-shaped sticks are not usually used by the modern pros—they have metal rods that perform much better.)

Even more important—the "magic" of dowsing is not the tool; it's the dowser. That seems obvious now, but when I first learned about dowsing (and TV didn't help here), I thought the tool was doing all the work.

As in any divination system, we human beings are the conduit through which the intuition flows. The teachers of dowsing are very clear that you need to "get yourself out of the way" in order to let the intuitive messages come through. What does this mean in practice? Clear your mind with meditation. Let all thoughts of ego, self, and desires recede to the background, and be open to the messages from Spirit. Let intuition guide the process.

The two most prolific authors and proponents of dowsing are Maggie and Nigel Percy. They have written dozens of books on the subject. Maggie and Nigel are particularly clear about asking the right kind of question when dowsing. Their most common tool for dowsing is the pendulum. A pendulum swinging back and forth is one answer (often "no") and going in a circle is another answer (often "yes"). But they stress how important it is to ask a very specific question.[9]

What can dowsers do? One of the most interesting is finding lost objects. Earlier, I described the story of *Extraordinary Knowing,* about the woman who got her daughter's harp back with the help of a dowser.

I have used dowsing with modest success to find lost objects. A few weeks ago, I was looking for a special pair of pliers that I had misplaced. After searching for quite a while, I decided to give the dowsing a try.

Beginning in the kitchen, I brought the pendulum into each room of the house and asked, "Are the pliers that I am looking for located in this room?"

Pendulum: back-and-forth. No.

Living room: "Are the pliers that I am looking for located in this room?"

Pendulum: back-and-forth. No.

Basement: "Are the pliers that I am looking for located in the basement?"

Pendulum: circular motion. Yes.

Ok, that's good.

At the workbench: "Are the pliers that I am looking for located near the workbench?"

Pendulum: odd wiggles. Not sure what that means.

In the storage room: "Are the pliers that I am looking for located in the storage room?"

Pendulum: back-and-forth. No.

After several strange wiggles in response, I decided to abandon the search for a while. Later that day, I found the pliers balanced in an odd position on the handrail for the basement stairs—something a nine-year-old child might do, yes?

I did get good information about where the pliers were *not* located, and I did have it narrowed down correctly to the basement. I probably need more practice in asking good questions and knowing what to do when the odd squiggly motion happens.

I found dowsing to be helpful, with even a minimal amount of practice. I can only imagine how much more effective it would be with some dedicated effort. I believe dowsing to be one of the divination tools that has the greatest depths to still explore.

Magic—Really?

When people think of magic, many different ideas come to mind. The slight-of-hand stage shows are one aspect. Then there's the goth and emo world with pentagram jewelry, black lace, and candles. Movies and TV love to use these images to either portray something evil or someone misunderstood by their peers.

But to *seriously* believe in magic—really? My friends in the sciences are incredulous at the thought.

One of my relatives tells a story of when her son ("Damon") was seven years old and really enjoying the Harry Potter books. For Christmas, he wanted a book on how to do magic. His mother bought a book of simple stage show magic, including card tricks, disappearing handkerchiefs and so on. When Damon read through the book, he was clearly disappointed. "These are just silly tricks! I want to learn actual spells!"

It's a funny story for everyone else in my family because they all "know" that you can't do spells and find his incredulity quite charming; however, I think the story is funny because Damon knows that spells are real (like me), and the rest of the family doesn't. We're in on our own joke together.

Dean Radin's book *Real Magic* looks at magic—the real stuff, spells, and causing things to happen—with more scientific evidence and even gives techniques for using magic.[10]

While I may be a "fan boy" of Dr. Radin, I want to stress how important and unique this book is. Radin takes the practice of magic seriously and analyzes how it might work. How cool is that!

He responds to the nay-sayers and science-only crowd this way: "Reality viewed through this lens of science is an exceedingly thin slice of the whole shebang. Science is tightly focused on the objective, measurable physical world. That focus excludes the one and only thing you can know for sure—your consciousness."

Science has its place—our amazing abilities to create new things, to understand how light and matter operate, to measure our world in extreme detail. The realm of science is truly amazing. But it is only a small slice of reality. Our own souls—our consciousness—is the reality that is connected to Spirit, to each other, to our intuition.

135

Radin makes that case that we are at the beginning of a new kind of understanding, that of the "psychophysical nature of reality." As we learn more about intuition and "knowing things," being able to see from afar, and seeing the future, we are contributing to a new knowledge base. If you are on the path of woo-woo, you are at the forefront of this knowledge!

Radin takes a good portion of the book to propose a possible "science of magic." Given that we have evidence for magic working, how might that be happening? What forces or conscious connections might be working underneath to allow magic to work? Radin has a few good theories, and pages of fascinating discussion on this topic.

Radin provides the following quote in his book:

> "The first stage is when you totally believe in witchcraft.
>
> The second is when you realize that it's a complete lot of rubbish.
>
> The third is when you realize that it's a complete lot of rubbish; but somehow it also seems to work."
>
> – Ronald Hutton[11]

There is a lot of truth in this quote; many people follow this trajectory in their lives. Kids and young adults dabble in what they believe are spells and rituals but then later they "grow up" and conclude they weren't real. And then… a little further down the road, they may begin to realize that somehow the rituals *do* seem to work, and there is a reality to this stuff after all.

In brief, Radin describes magic as an intent plus a ritual. He says, "The essence of magic boils down to the application of two ordinary mental skills: attention and intention. The strength of the magical outcome is modulated by four factors: belief, imagination, emotion, and clarity."

The best way to achieve the state of mind needed to bring this about is meditation.

Are you surprised?

Radin provides a lot of detail on the process of doing magic, some very practical step by step instructions, and much explanation of what the essence of magic is. He is clear on which parts are essential and which parts are just theater.

Even though I had been on my woo-woo journey for several years, I didn't take magic seriously until I read this Radin book. Until then, I had understood that woo-woo was a connection to the divine, that I could receive messages from Spirit and get answers to questions through intuition, but I could not affect the physical world. Now I understand it is even deeper and more amazing than I had thought.

Magic—Yes, Really

Imagine for a moment that magic is actually something that occurs naturally in the world, and we—the general population—are just now becoming aware of it. Magic has been part of stories and legends for thousands of years. Modern readers dismiss storybook magic as superstition, but now imagine if some of the magic in those stories is real.

What if the ideas of connecting with Spirits, communicating with your mind, and causing things to happen by means of an intent and a ritual—what if these are natural occurrences and we can learn how to do them, and use them in our lives? Wow. That would not only show that woo-woo is real, but it would open up the whole world to be a new magical (literally) reality!

If there is one practice I need to hone and go deep into, it is the study of magic.

Rupert Sheldrake on Dogs and Morphogenic Fields

Let's bring our controversial scientist, Rupert Sheldrake, back into the conversation. As you may recall, Sheldrake is extremely outspoken and very willing to present heretical theories in science journals. Like Radin, Sheldrake believes in our true nature of consciousness and our abilities to communicate and affect matter with our minds. In another one of his books, *The Presence of the Past,* Sheldrake presents his theory about how magic might work, called morphogenic fields.[12]

Morphogenic fields are like a well-worn path through the woods. The more times you walk on the path, the easier it gets to walk on that path. The more times an action is done, the stronger the morphogenic field becomes. A working magical spell is not one you invented today; a good spell is one that has been done thousands or millions of times before. The imprint of doing that spell is the morphogenic field. It works today because it's been done a million times before.

Sheldrake's theory explains a lot of how magic works and how psychic abilities work. As a scientist, he is experimenting and drawing from other experiments and other theories. But he refuses to shy away from woo-woo topics that other scientists tend to avoid. He is often criticized by the scientific community for being "unscientific" because of his interest in esoteric topics. But he rightly points out that the scientific community has put blinders on when it comes to studying woo-woo topics because of the scientifically accepted belief "that can't possibly be true." Both Sheldrake and Radin equate the modern scientific community with the Church in the Middle Ages—both organizations held fast to beliefs that the world must be a certain way, and any challenge to that belief was wrong. Both the church and modern science are held prisoner by the dogma and beliefs that must be adhered to.

The study of woo-woo is somewhat difficult because these phenomena happen through individual humans, who are notoriously flaky. One day the connection and intuition might be strong, and another day it might be difficult to connect to. Sheldrake's research uses a lot of anecdotal evidence.

In another of my favorite books, *Dogs That Know When Their Owners Are Coming Home*, Sheldrake cites hundreds of examples of strong connections between people and their dogs, between people and their family members, and even between people and other pets.[13] A specific story is one where a wife notices that 30 minutes before her husband comes home from work, the family dog goes to sit at the front door. They then test this action by varying his return time by hours, they vary his route, they use borrowed or rented cars, bicycles, or other modes of transportation, and so on; but the dog, without fail, knows when he is coming home. Even more interesting is that the dog moves to the front door at the time when the husband *decides* to come home.

The book is fascinating. Because there are so many examples, and the tests have been performed thousands of times with numerous individuals, I find it very convincing. Sheldrake does, too—he works the idea of morphogenic fields into his explanation of how this might be occurring. It's a favorite woo-woo topic of mine.

Acupuncture and Beyond

Once I was on my woo-woo journey, I learned to approach the world more magically. What has changed? I now understand that good things come to me naturally by a universe that has my best interests at heart. I don't worry about what happens in life. I have far less conflict with other people (and when I do, it's usually pretty easy to let it go). And I've learned so much about our bodies and health.

My first introduction to the woo-woo of bodies was when I lived in Taiwan for several years, long before I had truly begun the woo-woo journey. I was teaching English at a school in Taiwan. I had had back pain for much of my adult life at that point (I was in my late 20's) and had mentioned that fact to the school president's wife over dinner one evening.

She said, "Oh, let me take you to my acupuncture guy. He's an amazing Chinese doctor. He'll fix you right up."

I was very nervous about going there—acupuncture didn't seem normal to me, and I was worried about having this unknown person sticking needles into my back. But I did have the attitude while I lived in Taiwan that I wanted to experience the Chinese culture fully. If they did it, I could do it, too. (That also meant that I ate some unique dishes occasionally, but that's another story.)

The acupuncture and Chinese medicine doctor was very

knowledgeable and very kind. I got to experience "cupping" which is a method of using a series of small plastic cup-shaped devices placed on the back in order to determine where the body was most in need of care. Then once the cupping diagnostic was done, he inserted the tiny hair-width needles into areas along my back. It was very restful. I just had to lie there for a half hour to 45 minutes. Then he removed the needles, and I sat up with the back pain gone for the first time in many years. Even better, it stayed gone for weeks. I went for follow up treatments over the next few months, and each time the back pain was eliminated for longer periods of time. Finally, it was gone for good.

What *was* this strange magic? I was fortunate to experience acupuncture by a true expert in the field in a country that takes Oriental medicine and acupuncture very seriously. I was given the gift of an experience that affected all my future decisions about health.

When I moved back to the United States, one of the first things I looked for was an acupuncturist. Sadly, there were none in the city where I lived. Instead, I was introduced to a chiropractor. As you are probably aware, there are chiropractors who are serious about their study and want the best for their patients; and there are the kind who just want to make money quickly and see as many patients as possible through the day. My chiropractor was the first kind.

But he wasn't just a chiropractor. He was a practitioner of applied kinesiology, also known as "muscle testing." On my first visit, Dr. Ohlman did the normal chiropractic work of adjusting the spine. But he also did some muscle testing for supplements, based on my descriptions of having a stressful job and being very tired.

Muscle testing is where the practitioner puts something such as a supplement near your body (into your auric field) and then tests the body's energy reaction to it. There are a few specific tests that they can do to see if the muscles go "weak" or stay strong. If the supplement under test causes the muscle to go weak, that means your body does not need or want that supplement; if the muscles stay strong, it means the supplement is something that would benefit you. Muscle testing was discovered in the early 1900's, but studied intently and taught by George Goodheart in the 1960's. It has much to do with the body's energy fields.

I remember my first thought when seeing him do the muscle testing on me: "What voodoo is *this!?*" I understood acupuncture—stimulate a nerve, cause things to happen. But muscle testing was just too weird to believe. This was 20 years before my woo-woo journey began in earnest. I decided to play along—if he took care of my back with good chiropractic care, I could play along with weird energy voodoo.

Strangely, it worked. The supplements did help; I did get much less fatigued and stressed, and the care he provided was solid and effective.

I suppose I did, in fact, get a small taste of woo-woo early on.

Reiki and Energy Medicine

Many years after I first met Dr. Ohlman, he introduced me to a friend of his who studied similar forms of energy work. Jan was a Reiki practitioner. By this time, I was interested in the woo-woo body work—known generally as energy medicine. After resisting for several months, I finally decided I needed to experience Reiki for myself.

I was not disappointed. My Reiki session was calming and energizing at the same time. My mind felt very peaceful and rested, almost sleepy. But my body was buzzing or tingling with, well, energy. It wasn't a zapping kind of energy; it was a feeling of excitement and potential.

Around the same time, I began reading *Energy Medicine* by Donna Eden.[14] Donna Eden is one of the most well-known and accomplished energy medicine authors and teachers. Her story is remarkable. From a very young age, she could see colored glowing light around people she met. Happy people had clear colorful bands of light, and grumpy people had darker misty colors. She was surprised to find out that other people couldn't see the lights that she was able to see. She writes in her book about using those colorful auras to help heal others; her book is the culmination of years of work using energy to heal. (You don't need to be able to see auras to practice energy medicine, by the way.)

Donna Eden's books and courses quickly became my go-to for learning the woo-woo of health and healing. She and her husband David Feinstein have co-authored several books, notably *The Energies of Love* which teaches how our energy fields affect our personalities and relationships.[15] When two energy fields connect, as with people in a relationship, you can learn a lot about yourself and the other person by working with these energies.

What I learned from Donna Eden is that there are many things we can do on our own for our own self-care that are easy and effective. Her main book *Energy Medicine* has sections and lists of "What to do if you are feeling ____." If you have a headache, there's an energy routine to eliminate the headache; if you are feeling sad or depressed, there's an energy routine to soothe you and move your feelings in a more positive direction; if you have indigestion—yep, there's an energy routine for that.

I benefited immensely from Eden's Daily Energy Routine. It's a 5-to-7-minute routine of body motions designed to align energy pathways which lead to good health and vitality.

While I was reading Donna Eden's books, I found myself drawn deeper into Reiki. Reiki is a very ancient energy healing system but has much in common with other similar systems. Reiki has a very strong ritual surrounding the healing, including using special symbols that you draw in the air or imagine as you are doing the energy work. To become a Reiki practitioner, you must study under an existing Reiki practitioner; all (or most) Reiki practitioners can trace their lineage—the line of teachers—back to the original teacher Mikao Usui.

There are three levels of Reiki practitioners; in the early days the Reiki III Masters were very few, as students had to study several years and pay thousands of dollars to be allowed to take the Reiki Master class. Now that barrier has been eliminated, and Reiki courses are numerous and quite inexpensive.

Reiki as it is practiced today has its origin in Japan in the 1920's, but its roots are in Tibetan healing methods which go back many centuries.

The more I read about energy medicine and healing, the more I wanted to participate in this. I was intrigued by the ritual surrounding Reiki and wanted to learn. I reached out to Jan, the woman who gave me my first Reiki experience, and began studying with her.

After reaching my Reiki III Master level, I wanted to practice. By this time, I had a small group of woo-woo friends who were on similar journeys. We would spend an hour or two here or there practicing Reiki on each other.

The very best part of learning energy medicine is that you can share it. Either as a business of being a healer, or as a friend who wants the best health and vitality for your friends.

How Does this Energy Healing Work?

Many accomplished energy healers have written much about the body's energy field. The body has energy centers throughout, known as the chakras. There are seven main energy centers—the root near the pelvis, the sacral near the middle of the belly, the solar plexus right below the ribs, the heart, the throat, the third eye in the middle of the forehead, and the crown on top of the head.

There are also dozens of smaller chakras throughout the body—arms, legs, back, and so on. These energy centers are described in the ancient Indian medicine system of Ayurveda.

The ancient Chinese medicine system also works with the energy centers, but also traces the paths of energy throughout the body; these paths are known as meridians. Acupuncture works by stimulating or blocking the meridian energy pathways.

These and other systems describe the fields of energy that project from the body in layers or shells.

Reiki works by the practitioner's energy field connecting with and supplementing the patient's energy field.

Our current understanding of body energy combines the knowledge of chakras, meridians, and auras into a holistic system. Eden's energy medicine draws from ancient methods and systems, as well as more modern discoveries of applied kinesiology.

Diagnostic tools of energy medicine include muscle testing and the ability of the practitioner to feel or sense subtle changes in the energy field of the patient.

A malady or illness will show up in the energy field long before it shows up in the body. By using the diagnostic tools of energy medicine, you can feel where someone's energy is "off," and then using energy balancing techniques, meditation, or diet, you can get things back into balance.

How's that for a five-minute description of the world's most amazing health discovery?

Western Medicine

Does Western medicine believe all of this? No, but we're getting closer. Acupuncture is now an accepted and insurance-covered procedure. That's huge. Years ago, acupuncture was laughed off by many western medicine doctors as superstition or voodoo.

Numerous western medicine-funded studies on Reiki have all shown that it doesn't do any harm and improves patient outcome and mood.

That said, holistic energy medicine methods are going to be at odds with Western medicine's methods much of the time.

Dreams

A few months ago, I was working for a very difficult client, and wondering whether to end the working relationship. I struggled for months with unreasonable demands, micro-management, demeaning conversations with the client, and worse. One night, I went to bed with that difficult relationship on my mind, and then woke up in the middle of the night with a "download." I had dreamed of an entire five-point memo, complete with identifying the problems, potential solutions to fix them, and some creative ideas to make the working relationship better. I quickly scribbled down the points on my bedside notepad and went back to sleep. The next morning, I typed out the memo and sent it to the client who read it and took many of the points to heart.

Where did that memo come from? Was it just my brain working in subconscious mode? Or was it a divine message to help me get through the difficult times? To me, there's no question that it was a divine message.

Receiving divine messages through dreams has occurred throughout history. From the Greek myths, we learn of Morpheus, the god of dreams who can appear to mortals in any form and send them messages from the gods. The Bible has many stories of dreams that play the same role—Joseph in the book of Genesis has dreams about his brothers bowing down to him, and later Joseph interprets the dreams of Pharaoh.

In *Messages: Signs, Visits and Premonitions from Loved Ones Lost on 9/11* author Bonnie McEneaney presents numerous stories about people who had dreams of the 9/11 attack on the World Trade Center.[16] The dreams were of airplane crashes, fires, large numbers of people dying and other visions of what actually happened. Many people knew something terrible was about to happen, and many of them were people who died in the attack.

Most people believe that some dreams are premonitions containing messages about the future.

Of course, not everyone agrees on this point. In reading an article about premonitions of 9/11, the words of one skeptical scientist stand out. He dismisses the idea of premonitions as impossible:

> *"If premonitions are real, the most convenient way to explain them would be that information is traveling back in time from an event to a person. And so if that is right, then pretty much everything else we know about physics is wrong. That's kind of a big hurdle to get over."*[17]

This sentiment amuses me greatly. Yes, everything we know about physics *is* wrong, and yes, it's going to be a big hurdle to get over.

Physics has already come to terms with the phenomena (known as "entanglement" or "spooky action at a distance"), as described in great detail in Dean Radin's books. So, it's just a matter of accepting what has already been discovered.

One of the biggest problems people have in connecting to the divine is remembering their dreams. How can you get a divine message if you've forgotten it by morning? Deepak Chopra has a process that works very well to remember your dreams. In his book *The Spontaneous Fulfillment of Desire*, Chopra describes the simple process of "recapitulation."

The recapitulation process goes like this: before you go to bed, you review your whole day, reminding yourself of what you did in broad strokes. For example: I got up, took a shower, had breakfast, then did my writing, then had a Zoom meeting with Mike, then worked on the Hawkins project, then had lunch, and so on.

You take about five minutes to review your day. Then in the morning, you review anything you can remember about your dreams. After a few days, your mind gets used to the process of reviewing, and when you dream, the images and memories will start to be available for review. The longer you do the recapitulation process, the better it becomes, and soon you will be able to remember a great deal of your dreams. I have done this process and it works. It's quite remarkable.

I also read *Learn to Lucid Dream* by Kristen Lamarca.[18] This is an amazing concept and can bring you very deep into connection with Spirit. If the dreaming state is truly a potential connection with the divine, then knowing what's going on while you are dreaming *and* being able to affect the actions of a dream is a very powerful connection to be sure.

Lucid dreaming is exactly that. Lamarca explains that it's not about *controlling* your dreams; it's about being *creative* in your dreams. You have more choices open to you, and you can step back during the dream and say, "I'm dreaming, and this is a very interesting situation and I'm going to watch it play out."

Lucid dreaming provides a freedom unavailable elsewhere knowing that you are completely safe and cannot be harmed allows you to experience anything! The creative aspect of lucid dreams can carry forth into your awake time.

And the opportunity to resolve fears and solve problems is unparalleled. Plus, it's fun.

Lamarca takes us through a process of first learning to remember our normal dreams (using recapitulation), and then some steps to learn how to recognize you are dreaming. She outlines some steps you can take *in a dream* to confirm to yourself that you are dreaming. Isn't this amazing?

I have begun this process of learning to lucid dream, but I am still in the beginning stages. I probably need to get more sleep and be more rested overall in order to do this well.

Divine Communication

We can communicate with the divine using prayer and meditation. If we are paying attention, we can receive signs and messages from God, the Universe, Source. Tools for enhancing those messages have been around for centuries—tools such as Tarot, the I Ching, and dowsing. These tools are tools to enhance your own intuition and connection with the Spirit. The Spirit communicates through you, using your intuition. This two-way communication is unlike any other.

CHAPTER SEVEN

· ·

THE WOO-WOO COMMUNITY

Years ago, when I was working on enhancing my business, I learned about a mentor ("Gary") who was highly successful in getting his students to make their businesses successful using techniques of marketing and psychology. I contacted him, but he told me he was no longer accepting individual clients. My only option if I wanted to work with him was to join a coaching certification course he was creating with his wife.

I wasn't interested in coaching in the least, but I really wanted to work with Gary, so I signed up. The course was about 60% coaching material and 40% marketing and business techniques. Gary said that most coaches fail, not because they couldn't do the coaching but because they couldn't reach enough clients.

I learned a great deal from Gary, and that began my love of business and marketing; I have been using the systems and techniques I learned back then ever since.

But the real gold that came out of that course was the

community. In all previous online courses I had taken, the information was one-way. We'd log on, the instructor would lecture, we'd take some notes, and then we'd do it all over again the next week. But in Gary's course, there were weekly online lectures, and weekly online practice sessions with Gary's wife, Sharon, serving as the instructor. These were small groups, and the expectation was to participate fully, with audio on and a web camera on. This sounds obvious now, as most meetings on Zoom are exactly that. But back when this started (2014 or so), it was quite a new concept.

I remember the first practice session I attended. I assumed it would be just like the other one-way sessions. I had a microphone and a web camera on my computer, but both were off; I was dressed in an old T-shirt and was not in a place where I was comfortable talking, especially not role-playing a coaching technique. Plus, doing this all in front of a computer felt weird.

As soon as the session started, Sharon said "Hello everyone! Let's go around the room and see how everyone is doing! John, how are you doing today?"

OMG. I freaked out. What should I do? Come on camera? Try to talk on this "online meeting thing" while other people were all around me in the room? In a panic, I bailed. I quickly typed in the chat "Sorry, tech problems" and immediately logged off.

For the next practice session, I was ready—dressed decently, and in a private room where I could fully participate. It was a wonderful experience. I got to know my classmates and got to know Sharon very well. Over time, this became the best part of the course.

What came out of this "forced" conversation? I met the most amazing people in other cities and countries, some of whom are still my friends a decade later! Looking back, the benefits of this experience were equally business, learning the coaching techniques, and—most of all—the community.

The Tarot Community

As I learned more about Tarot, practiced reading with fellow students, and met more accomplished readers, I grew into the Tarot community. As with any passion, there are hundreds or even thousands of groups of Tarot readers. For some, it's a hobby, for others a full-time business, and everything in between. The Tarot community is a tolerant community—all genders, orientations, races, and opinions are embraced.

I was thrilled to get to know some professional readers personally. Through an odd series of coincidences, I met Melissa Cynova. In her words, "No, I manifested you, John." She needed tech help, and I was manifested to be the tech guy. We are now friends and business colleagues.

Two of my favorite books on Tarot, which I had read years earlier, are by Melissa Cynova—*Kitchen Table Tarot* and *Tarot Elements*.[1,2] I read *Kitchen Table Tarot* a half dozen times and got the audio book so I could listen in the car. Cynova breaks down the cards in a very easy to understand way—as though you're "talking at the kitchen table," and she also has wonderful stories from her past that illustrate her points. She is a lot of fun to listen to and is an amazing teacher.

Books are my comfort zone, as you might have guessed by now, but the next phase of my Tarot journey was actually an online class. One afternoon I saw that Radleigh Valentine, a well-known Tarot author, was offering an online Tarot course. I quickly signed up and began my Tarot journey in earnest. The most *amazing* part of that course was the community. The course would be partially lecture-based, but also involve Q&A sessions with Radleigh throughout the length of the engagement. One of the perks of joining the course was being invited into his private Facebook group. The most amazing part of the experience was this community!

Now, to be honest, I'm not a huge fan of Facebook, but I wanted to succeed in this course, and decided that participating in all of the course offerings would help me do that.

Was that ever a good decision! In the Facebook group, I met literally hundreds of other Tarot readers. Some were brand new beginners, just like me. But some were seasoned, long-time Tarot masters, who just wanted to help out, and participate in the community. One of the main purposes of the Facebook group was to facilitate setting up practice readings between members. The more you practice, the better you get—like any skill.

I received my first Tarot reading from a lovely reader from Estonia. We set up an online Zoom meeting to do our practice session, and she used a very unusual method (to me) of shuffling the cards until one card "popped out." She read that card, interpreted the meaning and then continued to shuffle for two more rounds. The reading was spot on— exactly what I needed to hear and answer my question in detail. I was very surprised and very excited to be part of this community.

Over the weeks and months, I was able to participate in dozens of practice sessions and honed my own Tarot reading skill.

Again, the best part of the Tarot course was the community. As we learned together, and learned about each other's lives and families, several of us became close friends.

To this day, most of the friends I now have in the light-worker Spirit-inspired world I met through that group. Some of my favorite people in the world are the ones I met through the Radleigh Valentine Angel Tarot online community.

Building My Own Community

There were about six or seven of us that were very active together in the community and became more closely connected. I know these wonderful people were brought into my life at the right time to help me on my journey. It's the woo-woo of community.

I had wondered for a long time about if and how we could meet for some kind of online party. I decided to give it a try and invited my close group to join in a Tarot Zoom party.

The Tarot Zoom party began as an experiment and now has become a regular event. Tarot readers and friends of woo-woo—both beginners and experienced pros—join the online event for an hour or two; we go around the room and each reader does a reading for one other person in the group. The conversations are always rich and full of care for each other. We learn about the cards, we learn about meanings, we debate interpretations, we participate in a safe space. But most of all, we belong. It's not a formal group with membership rules or bylaws. It's a small community of friends of woo-woo.

The Local Woo-woo Community

My other connection to the woo-woo community is a small group that got started to help woo-woo business owners to make their businesses better. Because of my long history of running a tech business, I have learned some best practices for business. Many business owners in this space struggle with the marketing or the daily operations of the business.

I thought—what if we could get a group of us together to discuss our difficulties and how we might best solve them? I wanted to help the local woo-woo crowd, so this group met in person. Once per month, we met to discuss a chosen business topic, held a Q&A session, and talked about the things we had learned.

Again, the business topics were interesting and helpful, but the best part about the forum was the community. The people who joined the forum are still some of my dearest friends. If you've never been in a room with a dozen other psychics, Reiki practitioners and Tarot readers, you have never experienced the buzzing energy like this! I would leave these meetings on fire!

Go Out and Teach

Have you learned a thing or two about woo-woo? Ok! Now it's time to start teaching others!

Teaching doesn't have to be formal or need official approval from a higher authority. I hereby grant you the right to teach what you have learned!

Have you learned something about *loving what is*? About happiness? About connecting with Spirit or something about reading Tarot? Bring your friends into the conversation.

Start with friends who have similar understanding and attraction to woo-woo.

Teach Online

Since I have a strong background in technology, I have found building things online to be straightforward. If you've grown up with websites, social media, Google and online culture, you will be familiar with the kind of technology you need to teach online.

The simplest way to teach online is to gather a group of like-minded online friends (from all over the world), set a date and time to come to a Zoom call, and say what you want to say. Make it interactive. Debate ideas. Think through the difficult questions. Hone your message.

If you want to go deeper into teaching online, you will want to reach people you haven't met yet. That involves getting the word out there about what you do—in the business world, that's called marketing, but here we can just call it "spreading the word about what you do." You can make your teaching your business or just your passion. There are many tools and systems that will help you build online lessons, video courses, track students, take payments and so on. The most important thing is to start! Start simple and build from there.

What Spirit Says

One final time, each of our three psychics asked the following questions of Spirit and channeled the answers from the other side. In this section, I asked about interacting with Spirit in the physical world, from healing to building community.

Here's what Spirit says.

Angie
Channeling Spirit Guides, Including Matthew

Q. Can we affect the world around us?
A. Oh yes. The energy you emanate has an effect on the world around you. You spread the light by simply walking in it. You manifest through action! Choose how you will affect

the world. Choose to support Mother Earth through your actions. Pray that Mother Earth does not get fed up with human destruction. Lead by example. Make your mark. Nothing is insignificant. Small changes add up. Bless your spaces, bless your journeys, bless your actions so that the way you move through the world emanates and spreads the light. Tune in to your environment and choose happiness, watch the energy shift. Tune into your environment and choose anger or disdain. Watch the energy shift. Which do you prefer?

Q. Can we help ourselves and others heal bodily diseases and maladies?

A. Some of you are more suited to this than others. The art and idea of healing is a complex situation, and it requires many things to be combined in a synergistic way. You can all help yourselves heal through prayer and belief. You can help others as a healer to arrive in that state where a person's body remembers how to heal itself. There is no one concrete answer to this. Whether or not a human can heal others in a grand way is determined by the story of their soul. There are as many different types of souls as there are different types of humans. So, dear one, the answer to this question is yes to some, and no to others. Success is not related to "goodness" or "badness," it is related to frequency. Frequency is related to soul song. Soul songs are as individual as a fingerprint.

Q. How can we help others who are also on this Spiritual quest?

A. By meeting them where they are.

Q. How do we build a supportive community of like-minded Spiritual seekers?

A. Ahhhh. Here is a good question, but one without an easy answer. There are many things to set aside to create such a community. Fear, judgment, and the collective consciousness to some degree. How do you find those people? At first, you might find one. Or two. Then as a small group, you set an intention and create a beacon to call others. When others arrive, you create another beacon to awaken others to the cause. This is a human construct that must be created organically. It must be managed with discernment. But it must also be open to new thoughts and ideas. A place to learn and grow.

Q. How can we teach others about what we have learned?

A. By doing. Teach. Leading by example. Sharing what you have learned. Practicing what you have learned. There is nothing revolutionary here. You must speak, write, and act in a place where others can listen, read, and watch.

Rev J and PESHMA

Q. What we can learn from Spirit and what we can receive in terms of signs from Spirit? How do we learn to communicate with Spirit? What's the best thing I can do to help someone else learn to communicate with Spirit?

A. What a beautiful question. So, the easiest way to help one to understand connections and bringing in the feeling aspect of the vibration is to use tangible things. Although Spirit is intangible, humans like to feel, touch, smell, use their senses, kinetics in order to be able to feel. And so, you start with the tangible and then are able to move to the intangible or not seen.

For example, if you wanted to teach a child about the Spirit of joy—which is Spirit in itself—perhaps you would show something physical. We would show a sunflower or a flower, a beautiful flower, something that you can hold, you can smell. When you do that, it brings you joy. You see a person's face light up; you see them shift.

That is just frequency, energy, flower. And it's a tangible thing. Then you put the flower to the side, and you take somebody into their mind's eye and say, "Bring that image of your favorite flower up. How does that feel? Where do you feel it? Do you get the tingles? Do you come to a memory that makes you happy and joyful and field of love?" That is basically what Spirit is, or the Spiritual experience is love and light and joy and all those other higher vibrations.

You start with something like that and move it towards them having that frequency that they've brought into their physical frequency. And from there you can move on to other exercises.

Q. What are signs that Spirit might give us along the way that might indicate that we pay attention or what are signs that we would receive from Spirit typically?

A. Well, they are all around you, of course. And they could be as mystical as finding an old feather or a coin to thinking wow, I'm having a really crummy day and you look up to the sky and you see a cloud in a heart shape. It's a matter of becoming aware of what is around you. But it could also just be a sudden burst or feeling of "Oh, I feel really happy today," or "I feel really joyful," or just an emotion that just comes into the human body. "I feel the Spirit in me."

It's a matter of one really using all of their senses and having all of their eyes open to be able to see, sense, feel that which is around them. It can be as simple as even a commercial saying a certain word or a song that comes on that reminds you of this time or that person. So, it's a matter of just becoming aware because the signs are everywhere. Just the simple nature's breeze on one's face is a sign. There is a song: "Sign, sign, everywhere a signs." It's just a matter of one opening up and receiving them, feeling them, seeing them and having the faith, trust and acceptance that that is what it is.

Q. Is it possible with Spirit to affect the physical world around us? (This is known as magic.)

A. Absolutely. Again, if you take away the physicality of the body you are left with frequency, energy, sound and light. And so, these are the things that make up your earth plane and your human experience. So, there is magic happening around every day, it's just not called magic. And look at the changes that are going on. Look at a child who has not been fully through mindful separation and the joy of the magic that they show in their lives with just even the littlest of things, the magic of being able to walk, talk, all of that is magic.

Using that frequency of words such as you are doing in these writings that you are doing and all the research that you have been doing will affect the change. And you will see more and more those coming into accepting of these words because that's all they are— just words. There are things that are going on even today that are miracles or magic and yet it's just the frequency of the word that sometimes off-puts others who might not understand or be in their awareness at the moment.

As more and more children are being born, you will see that more and more, that words such as magic or alchemy or those woo-woo words, so to speak, will be more mainstream and accepted.

Q. Specifically on health, what can we do to help ourselves heal our bodies and our diseases by means of Spirit?

A. This is a very loaded question, and this is where our speakings may be a little controversial to what is being said today. There is really nothing wrong, so to speak. It's just the language and the idea that if something is not functioning purely in the body—whatever purely is—that there is something wrong with the person. Perhaps they did not resolve trauma or they're going through energy attacks or fill in the blank. The human body is a fragile state of frequency, sound and energy coming together. And like anything that comes into physical form, it is not always brought in perfect. And imperfections are where beauty lies.

For a person who has disease, perhaps that was their calling when they came onto the Earth plane in order to learn more or even perhaps advance science or Spirituality. And there is a purpose for those who are in those lessons and to understand that imperfection is perfect. As you know, that is one of the sentences that Rev J uses: "I'm healthy, whole and complete despite my circumstances."

Because of her circumstances she has been able to have Spiritual experiences beyond her comprehension at times. And so sometimes these imperfections come in in order to advance science, to advance the person's Spirituality or lessons that they chose to learn in their life cycle and to be able to really learn that everything is just an illusion anyway. We sometimes feel saddened of how much emphasis is being placed on having a body that is free of disease, pain, inflammation, fill in the blank, and that one may be doing something *wrong* or they have not cleared their trauma. We are saddened by the assumption that if they would just do this, this and this, they would be healed.

We know that Rev J has done almost every possible thing that she can do to heal that which she is challenged with. And she finally came to the acceptance and realization of what we were saying to her. That in order for her to have a platform to reach those who are in similar states, to understand that you are love, you are light, you are perfect just the way you are, that there is nothing wrong with you, that (is the state) she needs to be in.

This is a very important question because there are so many people on the Earth plane today who are either seen as, or they see themselves as, broken or "I'm doing something wrong" or "We love this one but I'm being punished." This has nothing to do with that. However, if they drop those lower vibrational words or happenings or feelings and shift even in a body that doesn't function appropriately, (they are) still worthy and still have much to offer because eventually every body breaks down.

Q. What can we do with our teaching to help others who are on a Spiritual quest?

A. I think the most important thing is to meet the person where they are. Because if one tries to…what's the saying? "Shove it down someone's throat," then that is where more and more separation comes and becomes disconnected. So, when you meet a person on their level, you can drop breadcrumbs or say things in different ways that meet them on their level and allow them to come into their awarenesses. We are thinking of a couple of friends that in the past dismissed Rev J (and it has been decades), but now they are coming into their awarenesses and asking questions and growing at their own pace. So, it's a matter of dropping little breadcrumbs. Or it's like inviting somebody over who you make a meal for. They may not like everything, and you say, "Oh, okay, well, that's fine, but would you like to just maybe try this?" And they may try it, and it may be like, "Oh, this is delicious. Yes, I would like to learn more about this, the recipe," and so forth. Or they may be like, "I'm not ready to try that right now." And that is okay. So, accepting a person where they're at is the best thing that any Spiritual teacher or leader or even friend can give. This is how a light worker can be towards a student or those who are maybe not ready to light their way.

And just being an example. When they see the light and love in your eyes and how you emanate that out, hey, I want that, what are you doing to do? What do you do that I can do to get me to that place?

Q. How can we become truly happy in our own lives? What is the one thing that helps us truly be happy?

A. Take the time when chaos is coming in and things are coming at you in a human way and you have that separation, just remember to come back into alignment. The unhappiness or the lower vibration is you forgetting who you are and where you came from. That mindful separation. So, it's taking the time to stop, drop and roll. Sometimes you just need to stop and draw. But taking those times to walk out in nature, feel the ground, hug a tree, look up to the sky, feel the breeze, will remind you and bring you into that remembrance of your light, your love and your joy. And that will help to continue to perpetuate the happiness.

Shelly

Q. How about signs from the Spirit? Clearly, if you're paying attention there's signs out there. What would you have people pay attention to?

A. Numbers. Numbers are always one of the top signs. Secondly, animal Spirits that show up on your path—totem power animals. Thirdly, music. When you get into your car and there's a song that catches your attention and then all of a sudden you hear it again within a very short amount of time. And you hear it again within a short amount of time. And it might be a song from the 70's. And you're amazed. It's not necessarily a popular song that they just play to put it in your head so that you like the song. It's a song that could be from any decade and it's usually one that is from the past that you haven't heard in ages, and then all of a sudden you hear that song again. "That's bizarre, I haven't heard that song in 15 years. Then all of a sudden again it shows up."

Fourth, dreams. There's a lot in dreams and I feel there's so many messages coming through in dreams now and our dreams are getting much more real. They're not as faint and fantastical as they used to be. They feel a lot more like you're *in* a dream. A lot of us get messages that way.

I think those are the main ones that most people would notice. The 11:11, 3:33, 5:55, 12:12—many sets of repeating numbers.

I always think of the 11:11's as the wake up calls or the gateways in which there's a nice open gate for a particular transformation during that time. Those are the main ones that people would see.

Sometimes people find feathers, sometimes people see a bird outside their window or butterflies, dragonflies, or so many things, it could be anything special.

Q. Tell me about healing the body. What can we learn about that?

A. Energy work? Energy work is not specific. You can use your imagination and creativity and use energy in so many ways that if you can imagine it, you can make it happen. And so, I do it all the time to heal myself. Not to say that I'm completely there yet, but I work on different body parts, and I have noticed differences in my own body just having done that.

I even think about some of these other healing modalities, where people get on the infrared bed and this and that. I feel like those tools are just, again, bridges to a point where we eventually won't need that stuff anymore.

We won't need crystal bowls. I don't believe we're going to need tuning forks and we won't need other tools. I just feel like for myself, I love having those things and the healing tools are fun to play with. But I think in the future, coming up, we're going to be doing a lot of that with our hands and with our energy. And I think that a lot of these things like the med beds and things like that, are just an interim thing.

And I think in the 5D world—well, first of all, nobody gets sick in 5D. We don't need that. So, all of this stuff is just a bridge, right? Maybe energy work in the future, like on our bodies, isn't even necessary. I don't know because those vibrations can exist in the 5D. I just think that maybe this is just an interim thing, the bridge time, the transformation time in which these things are so important.

Q. What advice would you give for those of us who are light workers who are trying to build a community?

A. I think it's going to be super important. There's going to be communities all over the world—groups of people. There's going to be revivals, so to speak, where people go and listen to people speak. And within those groups, they'll form communities. And it may also be a new financial system within each community. I think that they will have their own sets of rules and not necessarily following like a whole state or a whole country or I think that the rules are going to be different throughout different communities for whatever works for them. I see that their foods will come within their own communities. I see a lot of things will be looked at in a much more locally, so that's where communities come into play.

Q. What can we do to help bring more people into the fold, teach more people about light workers and the metaphysical?

If we're talking about how do we help those people we come across that are just starting, just know that newcomers are taking off at incredible jumps now, as opposed to the slower starts we saw in the past.

What's happening is an acceleration of higher vibration, helping people remember "who they really are." It's speeding up. In present time, there's a much higher acceleration. So, a person who just woke up years ago would a few years later be barely a beginner, but someone waking up now would be much further along after just six months.

There will be teachers who teach at all levels, but I think for beginners, they need to have the right teacher. And again, you just take them back to the easy stuff. Let's just start here. Let's just get some basic understanding and get started with meditation. Start with meditation. Let's talk about your body's energy system—let's just build some "energy balls"— simple beginner level work. Let's not talk about all this advanced stuff that isn't going to make sense to them, that doesn't help them today where they are. Advanced teaching *does* help those advanced students where they are. It's about making sure that you have the right audience or the student has the right teacher.

Q. I wonder if you had any last bit of advice for a newbie.

A. Meditation. That opens up the whole ability to connect with Spirit on a much stronger level and that higher self, and it helps burn some of the junk away and so that will help in their Spiritual development.

Really, meditation is key, and secondly, taking personal responsibility, that's a huge one—taking responsibility. We have to monitor ourselves in that respect; Are we morally accountable? I know this is a cliche, but it's true: who are you when nobody's looking? You're not going to get into the 5D that if you are not morally upright. If you're still holding on to deception in any way, if you're hiding things, you're not going to get there. But again, do we stress out about it now? We take responsibility for our actions, and we can let nature take its course, and then make conscious choices.

If you're still in deception mode, you can't go any further. And so you have to be truthful in everything you do. You must have the mindset of always helping others by being truthful.

The third thing is healthy bodies. Movement. Get the lymph moving in our bodies. Why? Lymph is where the toxins build up. And so, these little lymph nodes in our bodies fill up with poisons and toxins, and it just sits there because it requires muscle movement. And so, guess what? Where does cancer go? Yes, it's the lymph nodes, and it travels through the lymph system. This is so very important.

It keeps our cells working and clean, and it helps with all these different cellular functions. It helps with autoimmune disease. It helps with all so much and the poisons and toxins in our food and our water and our air. So why do we exercise? It helps your body move that out. It means something right now. You got the why. You've got to know why.

The Last Word: Why Community?

What's so good about being a part of this community? Friendship. Support. Sharing joy and happiness. Learning from each other.

On your own woo-woo journey, seek out others who are on the same journey and meet your new family. I've found it so enjoyable to have a group to get feedback on my writing from, to try out a new idea, to ask about something I want to learn, and to give and receive blessings from.

CLOSING: WHAT'S NEXT?

One of the entertaining online communities that I visit often posts a topic of the day and then encourages community members to post interesting pictures and stories on that topic. Recently, the topic was "Jobs or careers that are 'scammy.'" In other words, what kinds of jobs are set up to scam or swindle their constituents? Many shared were the obvious ones, such as telemarketing, time-share sales, and similar occupations. However, I was dismayed to see alternative medicine and psychics make the list and get so many supportive responses.

It is true that there are scams and unscrupulous people in our communities. I know that. We've got a ways to go to clean up the perception of what we do. Bad actors do need to be called out and shut down.

As I dug deeper into the comments on alternative medicine and psychics, though, the one thing that kept coming up over and over was "I only trust science." What does that tell me? That tells me that the misconceptions we've discussed here are strongly at play. That also tells me we need these tools now more than ever.

So, what have we learned about woo-woo together?

Perhaps a brief recap is in order.

Trust that Spirit is real.

Your soul is a real thing; in fact, it is the *only* real thing. You're a soul having an earthly experience. Lean into that, and know that your Spiritual guides, teachers, and angels are helping you every day from the other side.

Know that science doesn't have all the answers.

Remember this: *Don't believe for a minute that we've figured everything out.* Reductionist science doesn't have all the answers. Thankfully, we are starting to wake up and see reductionist science (the belief that we're just a brain in a body) for what it is.

Know that religion doesn't own the truth.

No one religion owns "the Truth." Translations are never perfect. There is so much to be explored. Our knowledge and practice of Spirit do not stand still. We are not here to judge others. We are here to live lives of joy.

Know that the Modern Culture Trap isn't inevitable.

What if there's a better way? For those tired of being anxious, argumentative, and cynical, for those struggling with our modern-day ills, often what's missing is a connection with a deeper purpose. Woo-woo is the expression of a deeper purpose.

You have the Principles and Tools to support your journey.

As you continue on your path, use the Five Core Principles to guide you:

- Know where happiness is (and isn't).
- Treat each moment as if you had chosen it.
- You are not your thoughts. You are the observer.
- Now is what truly is. Only the present is real.
- Give and receive love.

Remember all of the various tools available to you to explore and access along your woo-woo journey. Experiment. Explore. Have fun.

Why Am I Here?

One of the biggest lessons I have received during my woo-woo journey is that I am here to teach what I have learned. This message has come to me over and over in many fun ways.

Once, I got a text message from one of my psychic friends, Joanna, where she said, "I have a message for you from Spirit. May I send it?" Honestly, I had never received a text message from Spirit before, but I'm up for anything like that. I said, "Yes! I would love to hear it!" Joanna replied, "Ok, they're telling me you need to finish your book." Oh, wow. At that time, this book was just an idea and a few paragraphs. So, I made a commitment to finish it.

Not long after that, I had a reading with another friend, Jennifer. It was a longer reading, but much of it centered around continuing to work on a project where I would be able to reach many others with the joy and happiness I found through my journey. Another message of affirmation.

In my own Tarot readings, I received many reminders and much encouragement to continue on the path of spreading this message of joy, happiness and woo-woo.

You have the results of that work now, *The Woo Woo Book*.

And, so, I thank you for taking this journey with me. If I may leave you with one final thought, it would be this:

Be the light in a chaotic world.
Get better at connecting with your higher Spiritual self.
Experience the true happiness of Spirit.
Watch for signs and listen to messages.
Bring others together and spread joy.

Continue your woo-woo journey with book additions, resource guides and a workbook at www.woowoobook.com.

ACKNOWLEDGEMENTS

I would like to express my deepest gratitude to the following individuals whose support, encouragement, and expertise have been invaluable throughout the process of writing this book.

Kim Marsh of The Open Book Company, thank you for your unwavering belief in me and for always pushing me to strive for excellence. Your insightful feedback and constructive criticism have shaped this book into its best form.

Maria Wade, I am immensely grateful for your thorough and constructive feedback on the book. Your many hours of work were inspiring. Your meticulous approach enhanced the clarity and cohesiveness of this manuscript.

Shelly Schultze, your encouragement during this writing journey has been a source of strength. Your contribution to this book has been a source of joy and awe.

Jennifer Rachlin-Holbrook, your support and enthusiasm have meant the world to me. Your belief in this project and your words of encouragement have fueled my determination to see it through.

Angie ZXUH, I am grateful for your contribution and

continued support. Your dedication to helping others is truly inspiring.

To beta readers Jaymi Elford, Dawn Price, Rebeca Davila, Nicki Pappas, Sheila VanZile, Joanna Maragos Pantazes and Monica Dobbins—thank you for your friendship and valuable insights and many thought-provoking discussions. You all have been so helpful in refining my ideas and strengthening the core message of this book.

Rob Rice, thank you for your artistic expertise and your contribution to this project. Your support and encouragement have been so appreciated. You have been instrumental in bringing this book to fruition.

To all the individuals mentioned above, and to the countless others who have supported me in ways big and small, I offer my heartfelt appreciation. Writing this book has been a labor of love, and your contributions have made it possible. Thank you for being part of this incredible journey.

NOTES

Introduction

1   National Alliance on Mental Illness. "Anxiety Disorders." *Nami.org*, Dec. 2017, www.nami.org/About-Mental-Illness/ Mental-Health-Conditions/Anxiety-Disorders.

Chapter One

1   Radin, Dean. *Entangled Minds: Extrasensory Experiences in a Quantum Reality*. New York, Pocket Books, 2009.

2   Sheldrake, Rupert. *Science Set Free*. Deepak Chopra, 4 Sept. 2012.

3   Sinclair, Upton. *Mental Radio*. Library of Alexandria, 1951.

4   Halpern, Paul. "Einstein and the Mentalists." *Medium*, 30 Aug. 2020, phalpern.medium.com/einstein-and-the-mentalists-f7eec1ad2e21. Accessed 2 June 2023.

5   Martin, Joel. *Edison vs. Tesla*. Simon and Schuster, 3 Oct. 2017.

6   McMoneagle, Joseph. *Remote Viewing Secrets*. Hampton Roads, 2000.

7   Elizabeth Lloyd Mayer. *Extraordinary Knowing: Science, Skepticism, and the Inexplicable Powers of the Human Mind*. New York, Bantam Books, 2007.

8   Wikipedia Contributors. "Sola Scriptura." *Wikipedia*, Wikimedia Foundation, 1 Nov. 2019, en.wikipedia.org/wiki/ Sola_scriptura.

9   Ehrman, Bart D. *Jesus, Interrupted: Revealing the Hidden Contradictions in the Bible (and Why We Don't Know about Them)*. New York, Harperone, 2009.

179

10   Ehrman, Bart. *Digging Deep into Afterlife Journeys*. 29 June 2022, ehrmanblog.org/digging-deep-into-afterlife-journeys/.

11   Moorjani, Anita. *Dying to Be Me*. Hay House, Inc, 8 Mar. 2022.

12   Weiss, Brian L. *Many Lives, Many Masters*. New York, Fireside / Simon & Schuster, 1996.

13   Giesemann, Suzanne R. *The Priest and the Medium*. Hay House, Inc, 15 June 2009.

Chapter Three

1   Schucman, Helen. *A Course in Miracles*. Glen Elen, Ca, Foundation For Inner Peace, 1992.

2   *Kardec*. Directed by Wagner de Assis, Sony Pictures, 16 May 2019.

Chapter Four

1   Katie, Byron, and Stephen Mitchell. *Loving What Is: How Four Questions Can Change Your Life: The Work of Byron Katie*. New York, N.Y., Harmony House, 2002.

2   Moorjani, Anita. *Dying to Be Me*. Hay House, Inc, 8 Mar. 2022.

3   Katie, Byron, and Stephen Mitchell. *Loving What Is: How Four Questions Can Change Your Life: The Work of Byron Katie*. New York, N.Y., Harmony House, 2002.

4   Williamson, Marianne. *A Return to Love*. Harper Collins, 13 Oct. 2009.

5   Eckhart Tolle. *The Power of Now: A Guide to Spiritual Enlightenment*. Novato, Calif., New World Library, 1999.

6   Chopra, Deepak. *The Spontaneous Fulfillment of Desire*. Crown Publishing Group, 2004.

Chapter Five

1   Katie, Byron, and Stephen Mitchell. *Loving What Is: How Four Questions Can Change Your Life: The Work of Byron Katie*. New York, N.Y., Harmony House, 2002.

2   Hicks, Esther, and Jerry Hicks. *The Law of Attraction*. Hay House, Inc, 1 Oct. 2006.

3   Kornfield, Jack. *Bringing Home the Dharma*. Shambhala Publications, 6 Dec. 2011.

4   Hicks, Esther, et al. *The Teachings of Abraham*. Hay House, 1 May 2004.

5   Tolle, Eckhart. *A New Earth*. Penguin, 29 Aug. 2006.

6   "Suzannne Giesemann." *Suzanne Giesemann*, suzannegiesemann. com/. Accessed 2 June 2023.

7   Abraham, Spirit, et al. *The Astonishing Power of Emotions: Let Your Feelings Be Your Guide*. Carlsbad, Calif., Hay House, 2007.

8   Lynch, Margaret M, and Deanna Schwartz. *Tapping into Wealth*. Penguin, 10 Oct. 2013.

9   Hicks, Esther, and Jerry Hicks. *The Law of Attraction*. Hay House, Inc, 1 Oct. 2006.

10 Helmstetter, Shad. *What to Say When You Talk to Yourself*. New York, Gallery Books, 2017.

11 Elrod, Hal. *The Miracle Morning: The 6 Habits That Will Transform Your Life before 8Am*. London, John Murray Learning, 2017.

Chapter Six

1   Laura Lynne Jackson. *Signs: The Secret Language of the Universe*. New York, Spiegel & Grau, An Imprint Of Random House, 2019.

2   Laura Lynne Jackson. *The Light between Us: Stories from Heaven, Lessons for the Living*. New York Spiegel & Grau, 2016.

3   Wiggan, Jessica. *How to Read Tarot: A Modern Guide*. Althea Press, 2019.

4   Valentine, Radleigh. *How to Be Your Own Genie: Manifesting the Magical Life You Were Born to Live*. Carlsbad, California, Hay House, Inc, 2017.

5   Valentine, Radleigh. *Compendium of Magical Things*. Hay House, Inc, 4 Dec. 2018.

6   Dick, Philip K. *The Man in the High Castle*. Boston, Mariner Books, 2011.

7   O'Brien. (2018, August 10). *The Visionary I Ching: A Book of Changes for Intuitive Decision Making.* Divination Foundation Press.

8   C., & Chang, S. R. (2012, June 1). *The Clear-Cut I Ching for Beginners.* CreateSpace.

9   Percy, Maggie, and Nigel Percy. *Ask the Right Question.* Sixth Sense Books, 15 May 2015.

10 Radin, Dean I. *Real Magic: Ancient Wisdom, Modern Science, and a Guide to the Secret Power of the Universe.* New York, Harmony Books, 2018.

11 Radin, Dean I. *Real Magic: Ancient Wisdom, Modern Science, and a Guide to the Secret Power of the Universe.* New York, Harmony Books, 2018.

12 Sheldrake, Rupert. *The Presence of the Past: Morphic Resonance and the Habits of Nature.* London, Fontana, 1989.

13 Sheldrake, Rupert. *Dogs That Know When Their Owners Are Coming Home: And Other Unex.* New York, Ny, Three Rivers Press, 1999.

14 Eden, Donna, and David Feinstein. *Energy Medicine.* Penguin, 21 Aug. 2008.

15 Eden, Donna, and David Feinstein. *The Energies of Love.* Penguin, 4 Sept. 2014.

16 McEneaney, Bonnie. *Messages.* Harper Collins, 8 June 2010.

17 A.B.C. News. "Disaster Predictions: People Claim Premonitions of Sept. 11 Attacks, Japanese Tsunami." *ABC News*, 24 Oct. 2012, abcnews.go.com/US/sept-11-terrorist-attacks-japanese-tsunami-people-claim/story?id=17553825.

18 Lamarca, Kristen. *Learn to Lucid Dream: Powerful Techniques for Awakening Creativity and Consciousness.* Emerville, California, Rockridge Press, 2019.

Chapter Seven

1   Cynova, Melissa. *Kitchen Table Tarot.* Llewellyn Worldwide, 8 Apr. 2017.

2   Cynova, Melissa. *Tarot Elements.* Llewellyn Worldwide, 8 Mar. 2019.

GET IN TOUCH WITH
OUR PSYCHICS

Angie

Angie ZXUH, the creator of The ZXUH Experience, a session that is geared completely to what you need in that moment in time. Zen Xpands to Unlock Healing! The ZXUH Experience offers a respite from what can sometimes be difficult work. Allow your Zen to Xpand to create ease in your Spiritual and Healing journey.

Schedule an appointment: <u>angiezxuh.com/schedule</u>
Contact: <u>info@angiezxuh.com</u>

Jennifer aka Rev J

Rev J's passion is to bring messages of hope, love and healing via trance channeling her collective-of-light beings called, "PESHMA" and other spirit guides (The Gang). She is a Reiki Master and holds certifications in Hypnosis, Mediumship, Trance Healing, Ro-Hun, Color and Sound Healing, as a Crystal Energy Guide and an Angel Tarot Card Reader. Rev J is an Ordained Minister through the Church of Wisdom (Delphi University), where she earned her Bachelor of Science in Metaphysical Healing. She also holds a Bachelor of Science in Social Work and a Master of Art in School and Guidance Counseling for the Deaf (Gallaudet University). She is currently writing her first book about her experiences along with channeled messages from PESHMA and is working toward gaining her Certification in Transpersonal Hypnotherapy.

Website: www.revj.net
Email at: Jennifer@revj.net

Shelly
Shelly Schultze is a gifted psychic and renowned energy healer with a profound ability to tap into the unseen realms and facilitate transformative healing experiences. For many years, she was the esteemed owner of Crystal Earth LLC, a thriving metaphysical business that provided individuals with access to powerful crystals and spiritual tools. While Crystal Earth LLC has recently closed its doors, Shelly's impact on the spiritual community remains palpable.

Shelly Schultze 's legacy as a psychic and energy healer extends far beyond her former business. Her unwavering dedication to helping others, coupled with her exceptional abilities, make her a trusted and respected figure in the metaphysical community. Whether guiding individuals through personal challenges, offering spiritual counsel, or sharing her profound intuitive insights, Shelly's work continues to touch the lives of many, leaving a lasting impact on their spiritual journey.

Website: crystalearthllc.com
Email: sld@crystalearthllc.com

MORE WOO WOO!

Connect with John and continue your woo-woo journey at www.woowoobook.com
Download additions to the book, a free resource guide and a workbook to help you on your journey.